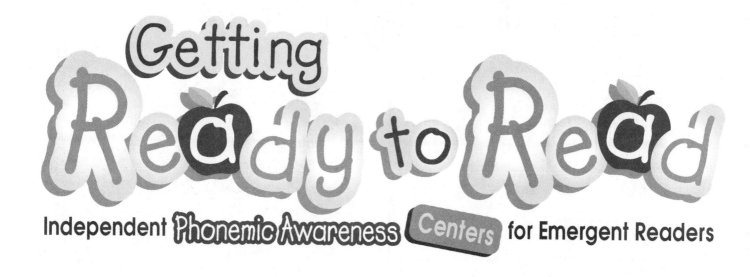

Getting Ready to Read

Independent Phonemic Awareness Centers for Emergent Readers

Written by
Jo Fitzpatrick

Editor: Kim Cernek
Illustrator: Darcy Tom
Cover Illustrator: Bernard Adnet
Designer: Corina Chien
Cover Designer: Corina Chien
Art Director: Tom Cochrane
Project Director: Carolea Williams

⋅*⭐ Table of Contents ⭐*⋅

✦★ Introduction ★✦

Children develop basic reading skills long before they are introduced to written language. As children learn to speak, they experiment with individual sounds and then connect those sounds to make words. Consequently, children do not understand the letter—sound relationship in written language until they learn to hear, reproduce, and manipulate the separate sounds within words (phonemic awareness). These skills are prerequisites for learning to read.

Getting Ready to Read directly addresses the phonological needs of preschool students, emergent readers, second-language learners, and other children who have not made these connections because of limited exposure to oral language. The center activities in this book help children learn how to analyze and apply the five levels of phonemic awareness (rhythm and rhyme, parts of a word, sequence of sounds, separation of sounds, and manipulation of sounds) in isolation before applying those levels to written language.

Getting Ready to Read offers over 40 center activities presented pictorially and in print. Children working at centers can look at the illustration on an activity card and immediately identify the requirements of the task. A self-correcting feature provides positive reinforcement and enables children to learn from their mistakes. Each activity also includes a card with clear, written directions for an adult volunteer to read in a small-group setting or for a parent to follow when you send the activity home for extra practice.

There could not be an easier way to help children develop a phonological foundation for reading. Simply copy the directions card, and gather the materials necessary to complete the activity. Then, introduce the activity to the class, model it, and place the directions and the corresponding materials at a center for children to explore on their own. At the end of the day, encourage individual children to take home the activity for some additional oral language practice.

You can maximize the value of the activities in this resource with minimal effort. As children in your class practice and master the phonological skills presented in this book, they will be *ready to read!*

⋆ ⭐ All about Phonemic Awareness ⭐ ⋆

It is important to understand what phonemic awareness is and how it impacts the way a child learns to read. Phonemic awareness concentrates on oral language and precedes phonics instruction.

What Is Phonemic Awareness and Phonics?

Phonemic awareness focuses on the sound units (phonemes) used to form spoken words. *Phonics* associates sounds to written symbols (i.e., the alphabet). Together, both forms of instruction help children develop critical word-recognition skills. Children can then apply the sound—symbol relationship to read print.

Phonemic awareness is essential because children must be able to hear and manipulate oral sound patterns before they can identify these patterns in print. Reading programs that include systematic instruction for connecting oral language to print lead to higher achievement in word recognition and spelling.

Why Teach Phonemic Awareness?

Children must first be able to hear the sounds and patterns in words before they can identify what letters represent those sounds. Therefore, children must be given extensive experience learning phonemic sounds and applying them repeatedly. Children who recognize the connection between oral language and print become successful readers. Phonemic awareness is the first essential step in this process.

How Is Phonemic Awareness Taught?

The goal of phonemic awareness is to help children hear specific sounds, identify sound sequence, and understand the role phonemes play in word formation. Phonemic awareness is basically oral in nature. Meaningful, interactive games and activities give children the best practice in phonemic awareness. Because phonemic awareness is multileveled and progresses through sequential stages, individual progress will vary and improve as children intermittently repeat a variety of activities at each level.

⭐ Five Levels of Phonemic Awareness ⭐

The activities in this book are grouped according to the following five developmental levels.

Rhythm and Rhyme

This level helps children develop stronger auditory discrimination and awareness. Level 1 activities give children exposure to and experience with hearing and identifying similar word patterns (sound matching) and listening for and detecting spoken syllables (counting syllables).

Parts of a Word

This level encourages children to listen for sounds within a word. As children discover that speech can be broken down into smaller sound units—words to syllables, syllables to onsets and rimes, and onsets and rimes to phonemes—they begin to blend these sounds together to form spoken words. Level 2 activities encourage children to identify onsets and rimes (syllable splitting) and blend individual sounds to form a word (phoneme blending).

Sequence of Sounds

When children reach level 3, they learn to direct their attention to the specific positions of sounds within a word. The activities at this level help children identify where they hear a given sound in a word (approximation) and identify beginning, middle, and ending sounds in a word (phoneme isolation).

Separation of Sounds

At this level, children are ready to acoustically divide words into separate sounds or phonemes. Level 4 activities help children count the number of phonemes in a word (phoneme counting) and identify individual sounds within a word (phoneme segmentation).

Manipulation of Sounds

As children reach this highest level of phonemic awareness, they begin manipulating sounds within words. The activities at level 5 give children experience substituting beginning, middle, and ending sounds of a word (phoneme substitution) and omitting beginning, middle, and ending sounds of a word (phoneme deletion).

⋆✶★ Getting Started ★✶⋆

Each activity in this book has three different sections, including a self-correcting feature that allows children to check their work independently. Read the information below to learn how to prepare an activity for use in a center or to be sent home for extra practice.

Section One

The top of the activity page features the level, title, and task involved in the activity, a list of materials, and the directions for preparing the activity and applying the self-correcting feature. Cut apart this top section, and retain it for your own reference. Copy the reproducibles on card stock, and laminate them for durability. Make a few extra sets of cards, and keep them on hand in case some of these materials become lost or damaged.

Section Two

The activity directions for a parent or adult volunteer to read appear in the middle of the page. Cut apart this middle section, and place the directions in a large envelope along with the materials for the activity.

Section Three

An illustration that shows children how to independently complete the activity appears at the bottom of the activity page. Cut apart this bottom section, and tape or glue it to the front of the envelope that contains the directions and materials.

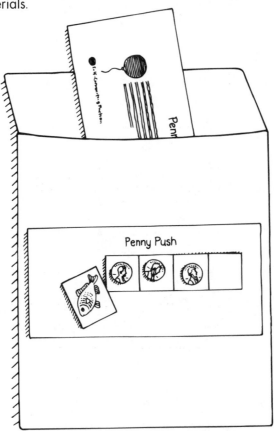

Rhyming Chain
Task: rhythm and rhyming

Materials
☆ Rhyming Chain Cards (pages 8–9)
☆ scissors
☆ hole punch
☆ plastic links
☆ paper lunch sack (optional)

Preparation

Copy the Rhyming Chain Cards. (Each page includes two sets of six cards.) Cut apart the first six cards, write the same number on the back of each card, and laminate the cards. Repeat this process with the remaining three sets of cards. Punch a hole before and after the picture on each card.

Rhyming Chain

Scatter the cards faceup on a flat surface. Invite a child to find two pictures of words that rhyme and attach the cards with a plastic link. Tell the child to continue linking other rhyming cards until he or she has linked six cards. Invite the child to find two different pictures of rhyming words and begin a new chain. For play with two or more children, give each player a different rhyming picture card and place the remaining cards in a paper sack. Have one player draw a card. If the card rhymes with the card in his or her hand, that player may use a link to attach the cards together and take another turn. If the card does not rhyme with the card in his or her hand, the player places the card back in the sack and passes it to the next player. Tell children to continue playing until each child has attached six rhyming cards.

❶ Self-Correcting Feature

There is a number on the back of each card. Cards with the same number belong in the same chain.

Getting Ready to Read © 2002 Creative Teaching Press

Rhyming Chain

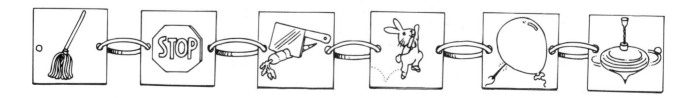

Rhyming Chain Cards

Rhyming Chain Cards

Getting Ready to Read © 2002 Creative Teaching Press

Out You Go!

Task: rhyming oddity

Preparation

Copy the Rhyming Cards, and cut apart the three cards in the first row. Note that two pictures rhyme and one does not (e.g., *pie* and *cry* rhyme and *pail* does not) and two pictures begin with the same sound (e.g., *pie* and *pail* begin with /p/ and *cry* does not). Decide whether you want the children to practice rhyming words or beginning sounds. Then, choose the picture that does not belong, draw a circle around the number below that picture, and laminate the cards. Repeat this process with the remaining seven sets of cards.

Materials
☆ Rhyming Cards (pages 11–12)
☆ scissors
☆ pocket chart

Out You Go!

How to play

Choose a set of three cards, and place them facedown in the first row of a pocket chart. Place a different set of cards in each of the remaining rows. Invite a child to turn over all the cards in the first row, and name each picture. Ask the child to decide which card is different from the other two and remove it from the pocket as he or she says *Out you go!* Tell the child to repeat the activity with the cards in the other rows.

❗ Self-Correcting Feature

The card with a circled number does not belong in a row.

Getting Ready to Read © 2002 Creative Teaching Press

Out You Go!   Out you go!

Rhyming Cards

Getting Ready to Read © 2002 Creative Teaching Press

Rhyming Cards

Full House

Task: rhyming match

Materials
☆ House reproducible (page 14)
☆ Rhyming Chain Cards (pages 8–9)
☆ scissors
☆ glue
☆ paper lunch sack

Preparation

Make four copies of the House reproducible. Copy the Rhyming Chain Cards, and cut apart the first six cards. Write the same number on the back of each card and one house. Glue one of the cards to the roof of the house. Laminate the house and the cards, and place the cards in a paper lunch sack. Repeat this process with the remaining three sets of cards and houses.

Full House

How to play

Place each house faceup on a flat surface, and ask a child to name the picture on the roof of each house. Invite the child to draw a card from the paper sack, name the picture on the card, and place the card on the house with the rhyming picture. Have the child continue to draw cards and place them on the correct house. For play with two or four children, give each player a pair of houses or a single house. Ask a player to draw a card. If the picture on the card rhymes with the picture on the roof of his or her house, the player may place the card on his or her house. If the picture on the card does not rhyme with the picture on the roof of his or her house, the player places the card back in the sack and passes it to the next player. Have children repeat this process with the remaining cards.

❶ Self-Correcting Feature

There is a number on the back of each card and each house. The number on each house indicates which cards should go on that house.

Getting Ready to Read © 2002 Creative Teaching Press

Full House

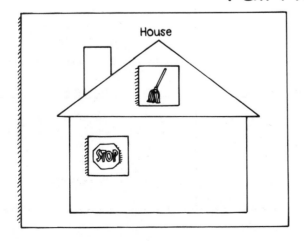

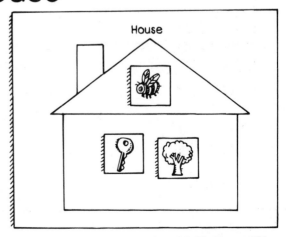

House

Rhyming Concentration
Task: rhyming match

Materials
☆ Rhyming Cards
  (pages 11–12)
☆ scissors

Preparation
Copy and cut apart the Rhyming Cards, and laminate them.

- -

Rhyming Concentration

How to play

Invite two to four children to play this game. Place the cards facedown in a grid. Invite the players to take turns turning over two cards at a time. If the pictures on the two cards rhyme, the player keeps the cards and takes another turn. If the pictures on the two cards do not rhyme, the player places the cards facedown, and the next player takes a turn.

❗ Self-Correcting Feature
There is a number on each card. Cards that rhyme with each other have the same number.

Getting Ready to Read © 2002 Creative Teaching Press

- -

Rhyming Concentration

Go Rhyme!
Task: rhyming match

Materials
☆ Rhyming Cards
(pages 11–12)
☆ scissors

Preparation
Copy and cut apart the Rhyming Cards, and laminate them.

Go Rhyme!

How to play

Invite two to four children to play this version of Go Fish. Have a child shuffle the picture cards, place them in a pile, and deal four cards to each player. Tell the dealer to scatter the remaining cards facedown to create a "fishing pond." Invite the player to the dealer's left to ask another player for a card that rhymes with a card in his or her hand. If the second player has a rhyming card, he or she must give the card to the first player, and the first player may take another turn. If the second player does not have a rhyming card, the first player should "fish" for a card in the scattered pile. Play continues with the next player to the left. Have children repeat this process with the remaining cards.

❶ Self-Correcting Feature
There is a number on each card. Cards that rhyme with each other have the same number.

Getting Ready to Read © 2002 Creative Teaching Press

Go Rhyme!

Rhyming Tic-Tac-Toe
Task: rhyming match

Materials
☆ Tic-Tac-Toe Cards
   (page 18)
☆ Tic-Tac-Toe Boards
   (pages 19–20)
☆ scissors
☆ paper lunch sack
☆ game markers (e.g.,
   plastic counters,
   pennies)

Preparation

Copy and cut apart the Tic-Tac-Toe Cards, laminate them, and place them in a paper lunch sack. Make a few copies of the Tic-Tac-Toe Boards, and laminate them.

Rhyming Tic-Tac-Toe

How to play

Invite one or two children to play this game. Give each player a Tic-Tac-Toe Board and some game markers. Invite a player to draw a card from the paper sack, name the picture without showing it to the other players, and place it back in the sack. If the player has a picture on his or her board that rhymes with the card, he or she may place a game marker over only one rhyming picture on the board. Have players take turns drawing cards and marking their board until they cover three pictures in a row. Tell children to exchange boards, and repeat the activity.

! **Self-Correcting Feature**

The number on each card matches the number where it belongs on the board.

Getting Ready to Read © 2002 Creative Teaching Press

Rhyming Tic-Tac-Toe

Tic-Tac-Toe Cards

Tic-Tac-Toe Board

Tic-Tac-Toe Board

Snake Race

Task: rhyming match

Preparation

Make four copies of the Snake reproducible. Cut out the pieces, and glue them together along the tabs to make four snakes. Copy the Rhyming Chain Cards, and cut apart the first six cards. Write the same number on the back of each card and one snake. Glue one of the cards to the head of the snake. Laminate the snake and the cards, and place the cards in a paper sack. Repeat this process with the remaining three sets of cards and snakes.

Materials

☆ Snake reproducible (page 22)

☆ Rhyming Chain Cards (pages 8–9)

☆ scissors

☆ glue

☆ paper lunch sack

Snake Race

How to play

Have a child place the snakes faceup on a flat surface. Ask the child to name the picture on the head of each snake. Invite the child to draw a card from the paper sack and name the picture. Tell the child to place the card on the snake with the rhyming picture on its head. Have the child continue to draw cards and place them on the matching snake until no cards remain. For play with two or four children, give each player a pair of snakes or a single snake, and have players take turns drawing and placing cards on their snake(s).

❗ Self-Correcting Feature

There is a number on the back of each card and each snake. The number on each snake indicates which cards should go on that snake.

Getting Ready to Read © 2002 Creative Teaching Press

Snake Race

Snake

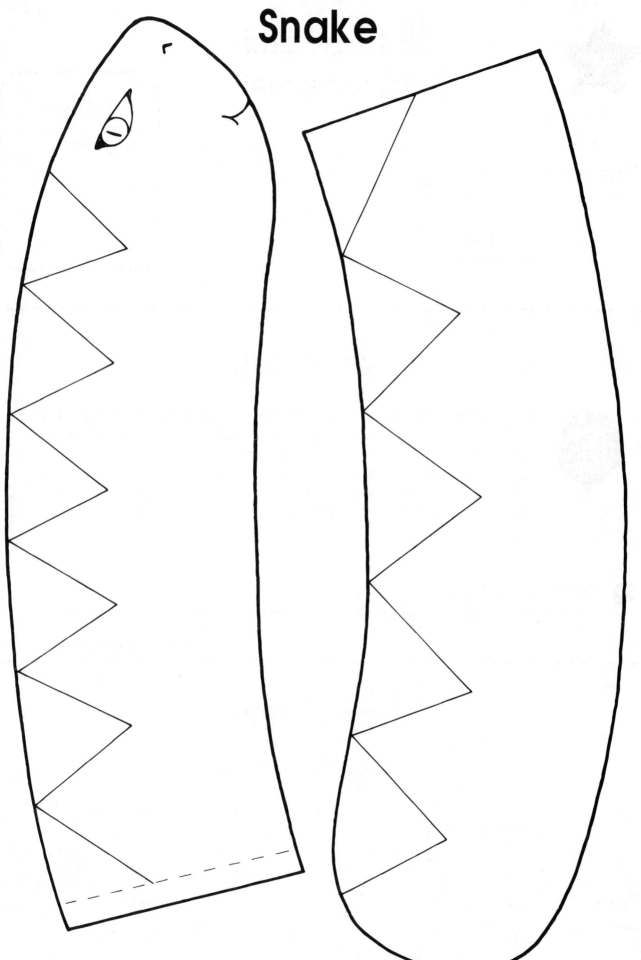

Puzzle Match

Task: rhyming match

Preparation
Copy and cut apart the Puzzle Match Cards, and laminate them.

Puzzle Match

How to play

Have a child place all of the puzzle pieces faceup on a flat surface. Tell the child to find two pictures that rhyme and fit them together to make a puzzle. After the child completes all ten puzzles, invite him or her to read aloud each pair of rhyming words.

❗ Self-Correcting Feature
Only pieces with rhyming words fit together to form a complete puzzle.

Getting Ready to Read © 2002 Creative Teaching Press

Puzzle Match

Puzzle Match Cards

Level 1

Flip-a-Rhyme
Task: rhyming match

Materials
☆ Flip-a-Rhyme Book reproducibles (pages 26–27)
☆ scissors
☆ plastic binding machine/binding

Preparation

Copy the Flip-a-Rhyme Book reproducibles. Cut apart the strips along the bold-faced lines, and arrange the strips in a pile. Bind the pile above the pictures on the top strip. Cut along the dotted lines on each strip to create separate cards. Turn over the book, and write the same number on the back of each set of three rhyming cards.

- -

Flip-a-Rhyme

How to play

Give a child the Flip-a-Rhyme Book, and tell him or her to flip the pages so that three rhyming pictures show at one time. Encourage the child to name all three pictures and then flip to a different set.

❶ Self-Correcting Feature

There is a number on the back of each card. The three pictures that rhyme have the same number.

Getting Ready to Read © 2002 Creative Teaching Press

- -

Flip-a-Rhyme

Flip-a-Rhyme Book

Getting Ready to Read © 2002 Creative Teaching Press

Flip-a-Rhyme Book

Rhyme Time

Task: rhyming match

 Level 1

 How to play

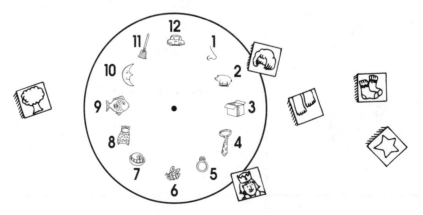

Materials
☆ Clock reproducible (page 29)
☆ Rhyme Time Cards (page 30)
☆ scissors

Preparation

Make an enlarged copy of the Clock reproducible and the Rhyme Time Cards. Cut out the clock, and laminate it. Cut apart the cards, write on the back of each card the number from the clock for the rhyming word, and laminate them.

Rhyme Time

Place the clock on a flat surface, and scatter the cards faceup around it. Invite a child to select a picture card and match it to a rhyming picture on the clock. Have the child repeat the process with the remaining cards. Encourage the child to name the pictures in each rhyming pair beginning with one o'clock.

❗ Self-Correcting Feature

The number on the back of each card matches the number of its rhyming word on the clock.

Getting Ready to Read © 2002 Creative Teaching Press

Rhyme Time

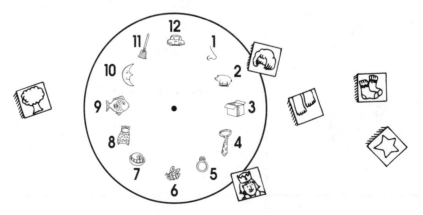

Clock

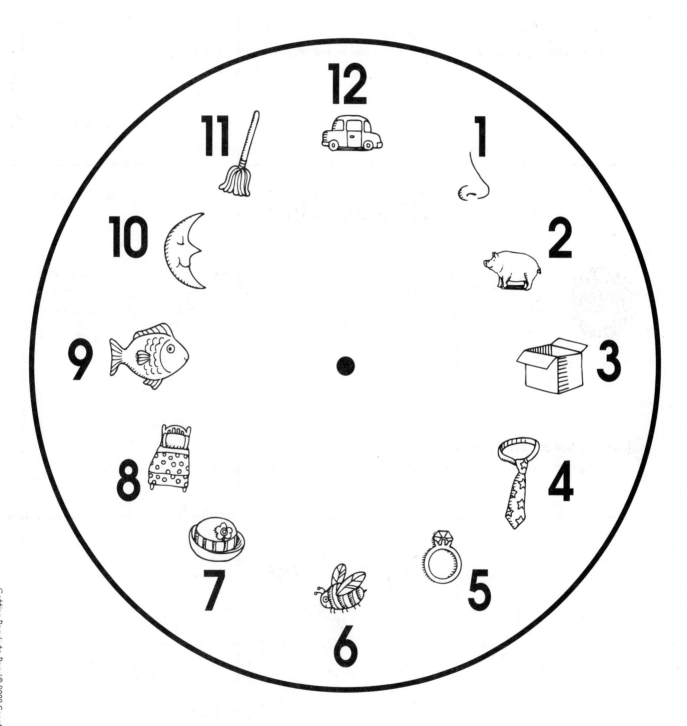

Rhyme Time Cards

Syllable Puzzles
Task: recognizing syllables

Materials
☆ Syllable Puzzles
  (pages 32–33)
☆ scissors

Preparation
Copy and cut apart the Syllable Puzzles, and laminate the pieces.

Syllable Puzzles

Have a child place the puzzle pieces faceup on a flat surface. Tell the child that two pieces fit together to make a picture. As the child completes a puzzle, have him or her slowly name the word for the picture to emphasize the separate syllables.

❗ Self-Correcting Feature
The picture will be incomplete if you assemble the wrong pieces.

Getting Ready to Read © 2002 Creative Teaching Press

Syllable Puzzles

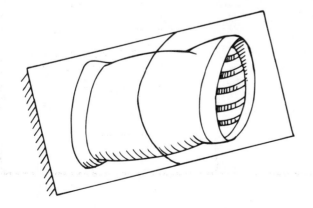

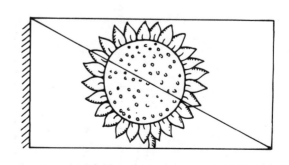

Syllable Puzzles

Getting Ready to Read © 2002 Creative Teaching Press

Syllable Puzzles

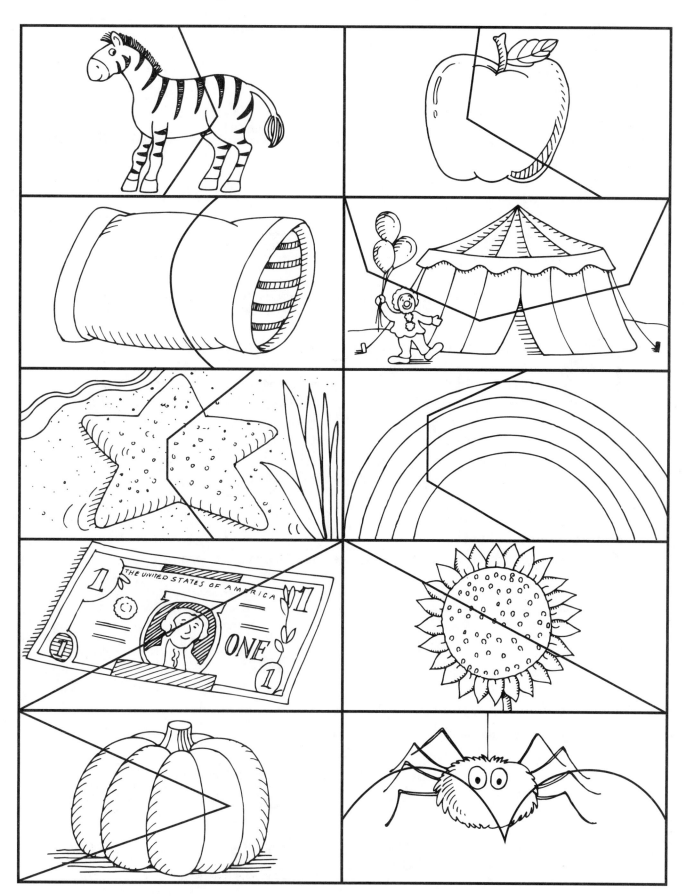

Syllable Race
Task: counting syllables

Materials
☆ Racetrack repro-
   ducible (page 35)
☆ Syllable Cards
   (pages 36—37)
☆ crayons
☆ scissors
☆ paper lunch sack

Preparation
Make four copies of the Racetrack reproducible, color each car on a paper a
different color (use the same four colors on each paper), and laminate them.
Copy and cut apart the Syllable Cards. Draw a small colored dot that matches
the color of the first car on the back of each one-syllable word card. Repeat
with the two-, three- and four-syllable word cards and their corresponding colors. Laminate the cards, and place them in a paper sack.

Syllable Race

Place a racetrack on a flat surface. Invite a child to draw a card, name the picture on it, and
decide how many syllables are in the word. Tell the child to place the card on the car with the
same number as the number of syllables in the word. Have the child repeat the process with the
remaining cards. For play with two to four children, give each player a racetrack, place the
cards faceup in a pile, and have players take turns drawing cards and placing them on their
racetrack until each car has a card on it. If a player draws a card with the same number of
syllables as another card already on a car, he or she should return the card to the bottom of
the pile. To increase the difficulty of the activity, have children play sequentially (i.e., they can
only place a card with two syllables if a card with one syllable is already on the racetrack).

❶ Self-Correcting Feature
The colored dot on the back of the card matches the car to which it belongs.

Getting Ready to Read © 2002 Creative Teaching Press

Syllable Race

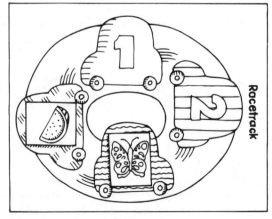

Racetrack

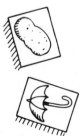

Racetrack

Syllable Cards

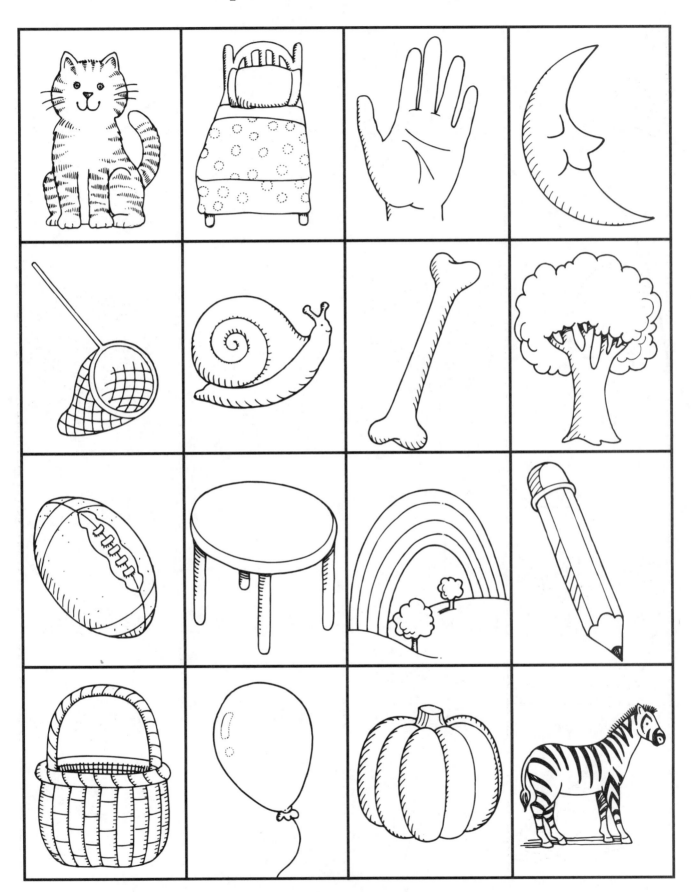

Syllable Cards

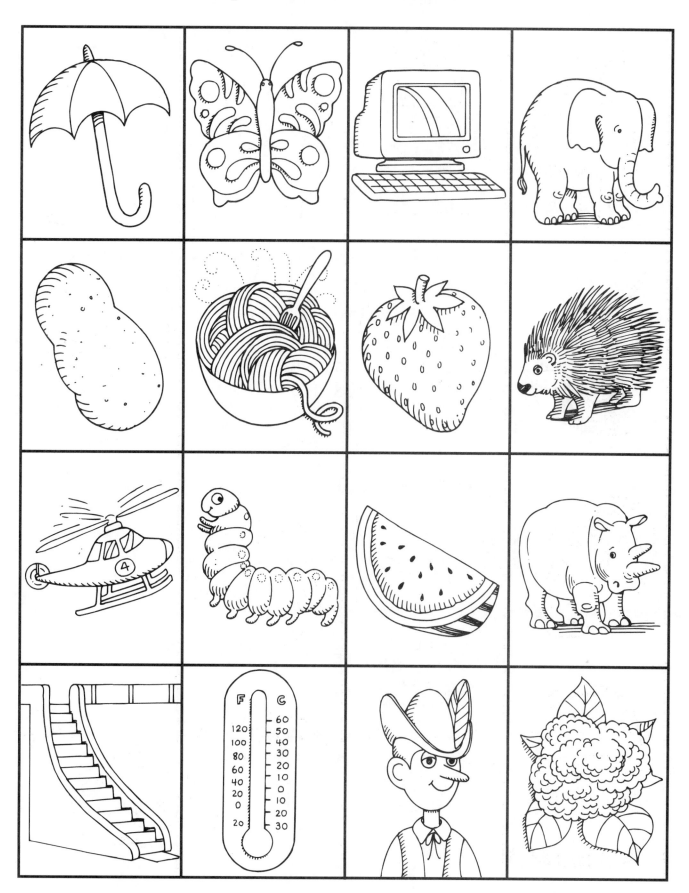

Level 1

Syllable Sort

Task: recognizing syllables

Materials
☆ Syllable Cards (pages 36—37)
☆ scissors
☆ crayons
☆ shoe box
☆ craft knife (optional)

Preparation

Copy and cut apart the the Syllable Cards. Draw a small colored dot on the back of each one-syllable word card. Use a different color to repeat the process with the two-, three-, and four-syllable word cards, and laminate them. Place the cover of a shoe box on a flat surface, cut in a horizontal line along the top four small slots that are the width of a card, and put the top back on the shoe box. Use the same color as the dot on the one-syllable word cards to write *1* above the first slot. Repeat with the coordinating colors for slots 2—4.

- -

Syllable Sort

How to play

Place the shoe box on a flat surface. Shuffle the cards, and place them faceup in a pile. Invite a child to draw a card, name the picture, and decide how many syllables are in the word. Tell the child to slip the card through the slot on the box that matches the number of syllables in the word. Have the child repeat the process with the remaining cards.

❗ Self-Correcting Feature

The colored dot on the back of the card matches the slot in which it belongs.

Getting Ready to Read © 2002 Creative Teaching Press

- -

Syllable Sort

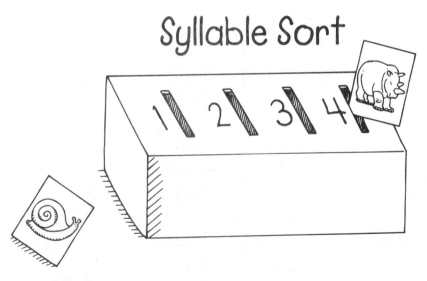

Graph It
Task: counting syllables

Materials
☆ Graph reproducible (page 40)
☆ More Syllable Cards (pages 41–42)
☆ tape
☆ scissors

Preparation

Make two copies of the Graph reproducible, and tape them together to make four columns of eight. Label below the bottom row of boxes from 1 to 4, and laminate the graph. Copy and cut apart the More Syllable Cards. Count the number of syllables in each word, and draw the same number of dots on the back of each card. Laminate the cards.

- -

Graph It

Place the graph on a flat surface, shuffle the cards, and place them faceup in a pile. Invite a child to draw a card, name the picture, and decide how many syllables are in the word. Tell the child to place the card in the column on the graph with the same number as the number of syllables in the word. Have the child repeat the process with the remaining cards. Ask the child questions about the graph, such as *How many four-syllable words are there?* or *How many syllables do most of the words have?*

❗ Self-Correcting Feature

The correct number of syllables is shown in dots on the back of each card.

Getting Ready to Read © 2002 Creative Teaching Press

- -

Graph It

Graph

More Syllable Cards

More Syllable Cards

Level 1

Tower Power
Task: recognizing syllables

Materials
☆ More Syllable Cards (pages 41–42)
☆ scissors
☆ paper lunch sack
☆ linking cubes

Preparation

Copy and cut apart the More Syllable Cards. Count the number of syllables in each word, and draw the same number of dots on the back of each card. Laminate the cards, and place them in a paper sack.

- -

Tower Power

How to play

Invite a child to draw cards from the paper sack until he or she picks a one-syllable word. Ask the child to place the one-syllable card and one linking cube on a flat surface. Tell the child to return the unused cards to the sack and then draw cards again until he or she pickes a two-syllable word. Have the child connect two linking cubes. Have the child place the two-syllable card and "tower" beside the one-syllable card and tower. Have the child repeat this process with three- and four-syllable cards. For play with two or more children, have the players take turns drawing cards in sequence and building their own towers.

! **Self-Correcting Feature**

The correct number of syllables is shown in dots on the back of each card.

Getting Ready to Read © 2002 Creative Teaching Press

- -

Tower Power

Link 'Em Up
Task: counting syllables

Materials
☆ More Syllable Cards (pages 41–42)
☆ scissors
☆ paper lunch sack
☆ plastic links

Preparation
Copy and cut apart the More Syllable Cards. Count the number of syllables in each word, and draw the same number of dots on the back of each card. Laminate the cards, and place them in a paper sack.

- -

Link 'Em Up

How to play

Have a child draw a card from the paper sack and name the picture on it. Ask the child to connect the same number of links as the number of syllables in the word. Tell the child to continue drawing cards and adding the correct number of links to the chain until no cards remain. For play with two or more players, have the children take turns drawing cards from the sack and forming their own chains until no cards remain.

❗ Self-Correcting Feature
The correct number of syllables is shown in dots on the back of each card.

Getting Ready to Read © 2002 Creative Teaching Press

- -

Link 'Em Up

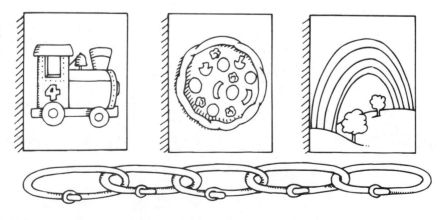

Onset/Rime Puzzles
Task: splitting syllables

Materials
☆ Onset/Rime Puzzles
(pages 46–47)
☆ scissors

Preparation
Copy and cut apart the the Onset/Rime Puzzles, and laminate the pieces.

Onset/Rime Puzzles

How
to
play

Have a child place the puzzle pieces faceup on a flat surface. Tell the child that two pieces fit together to make a picture. Have the child say the onset (all of the sounds in a word that come before the first vowel) and the rime (the first vowel in a word and all the sounds that follow) of the word for the picture, such as /b/ /ike/ for the bike puzzle, as he or she connects the puzzle. Have the child repeat this process with the remaining puzzles.

❗ Self-Correcting Feature
The two parts of each word fit together to form a complete puzzle.

Getting Ready to Read © 2002 Creative Teaching Press

Onset/Rime Puzzles

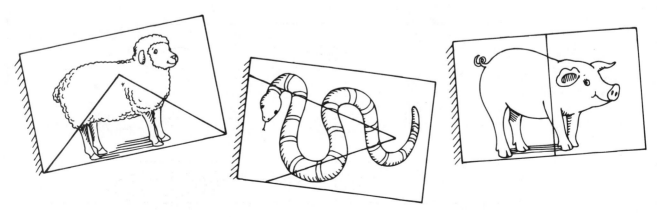

Onset/Rime Puzzles

Onset/Rime Puzzles

Say It, Take It

Task: splitting onsets and rimes

Preparation

Copy the Say It, Take It reproducibles. (Each page includes four sets of four cards.) Cut apart the first four cards, and write the beginning sound of the word on the back of each card. Laminate the cards, place them in an envelope, and write *1* on the envelope. Repeat this process with the remaining seven sets of cards using numbers 2–8.

Materials

☆ Say It, Take It reproducibles (pages 49–50)

☆ scissors

☆ envelopes

Say It, Take It

How to play

Invite two or more children to play this game. Give the group of players one envelope. Ask one player to shuffle four cards, and place them faceup in a row. Invite another player to look at the pictures on the cards and say the beginning sound of only one of the cards. Tell the other players to look for the card that begins with that sound. The first player to say the second part of the word and make the complete word wins the card. For example, the first player says /s/ and another player says /un/ to make the word *sun*. Ask the player who won the card to say the beginning sound of one of the remaining cards, and repeat the process. When no cards remain, have children repeat the activity with a new set of cards.

❗ Self-Correcting Feature

The beginning sound of the word is written on the back of each card.

Getting Ready to Read © 2002 Creative Teaching Press

Say It, Take It

 /n/

/ut/

Say It, Take It

Say It, Take It

Getting Ready to Read © 2002 Creative Teaching Press

Level 2

Word Family Fun
Task: splitting syllables

Materials
☆ Word Family Fun Cards (page 52)
☆ Letter Cards (pages 53–54)
☆ scissors
☆ envelopes

Preparation
Copy the Word Family Fun Cards. Cut apart the first four cards, and write the word for each picture and *1* on the back of each card. Laminate the cards, place them in an envelope, and write *1* on the envelope. Repeat this process with the remaining three sets of cards using numbers 2–4. Copy and cut apart the Letter Cards, and laminate them.

- -

Word Family Fun

How to play

Give a child a set of letter cards and an envelope. Tell the child to name the picture on one of the cards and use the letter cards to spell the word. Have the child choose a new card and name it. Tell the child that he or she will change one of the letter cards to spell the new picture word. Ask the child to repeat this process with the remaining two cards. Give the child a new envelope, and have him or her repeat the activity.

❗ **Self-Correcting Feature**
All cards have the name of the picture written on the back.

Getting Ready to Read © 2002 Creative Teaching Press

- -

Word Family Fun

   b **h** **m**   **c** **a** **t**

Word Family Fun Cards

Getting Ready to Read © 2002 Creative Teaching Press

Letter Cards

a	b	c	d
e	f	g	h
i	j	k	l
m	n	o	p
q	r	s	t

Letter Cards

u	v	w	x
y	z	a	d
e	g	i	l
m	n	o	p
r	s	t	u

Build a Picture

Task: oral blending

Materials
☆ Build a Picture reproducible (page 56)
☆ scissors

Preparation

Copy the Build a Picture reproducible, cut apart the strips, and laminate them.

Build a Picture

Scatter the strips for one of the pictures faceup on a flat surface. Have a child connect the strips to form a picture. Tell the child to slowly name the picture as he or she connects the strips. For example, as the child assembles the picture of the cake, he or she would say /c/ /ā/ /k/. Have the child repeat this process to make seven more pictures.

How to play

❗ Self-Correcting Feature

The picture will be incomplete if you assemble the wrong pieces.

Getting Ready to Read © 2002 Creative Teaching Press

Build a Picture

/t/ /r/ /ē/

Build a Picture

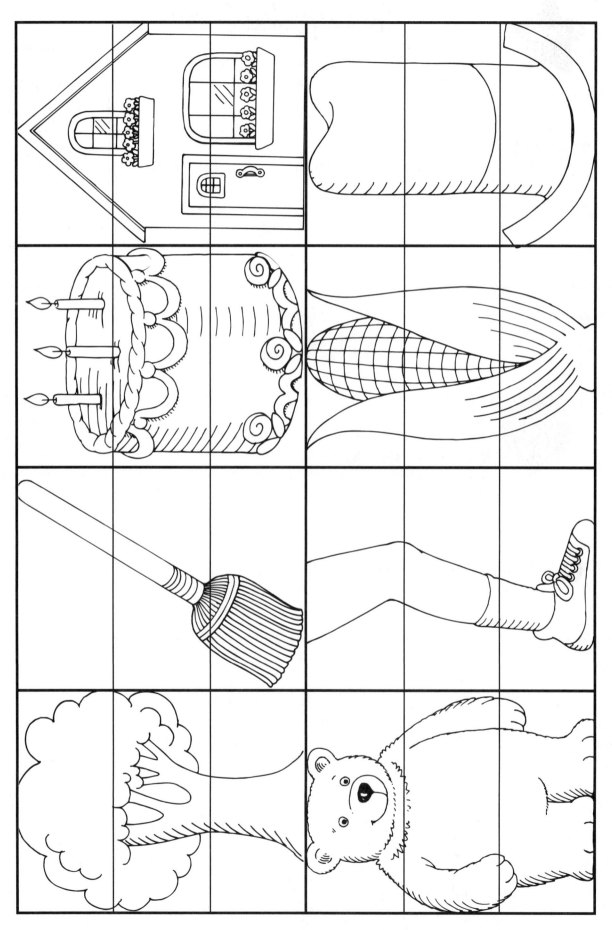

Level 2

Slowpoke Slide
Task: oral blending

Materials
☆ Slides reproducible (page 58)
☆ Blending Cards (pages 59–60)
☆ scissors

Preparation
Copy the Slides reproducible, cut out the slides, and laminate them. Copy and cut apart the Blending Cards, and laminate them.

- -

Slowpoke Slide

How to play

Place a slide on a flat surface, and give a child a set of cards. Have the child select a card and place it at the top of the slide. Encourage the child to move the card down the slide and slowly say the name of the picture while stretching out the sounds until the card reaches the bottom. Tell the child to repeat the process with the remaining cards. For play with two or more children, give each player a slide, and distribute the cards evenly between the players. Have the players take turns sliding cards and slowly saying the names.

❗ Self-Correcting Feature
The last sound of the word should be said as the card reaches the bottom of the slide.

Getting Ready to Read © 2002 Creative Teaching Press

- -

Slowpoke Slide

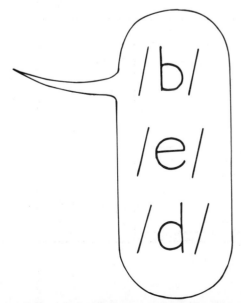

/b/
/e/
/d/

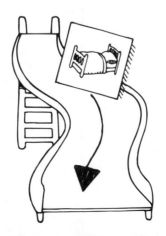

Slides

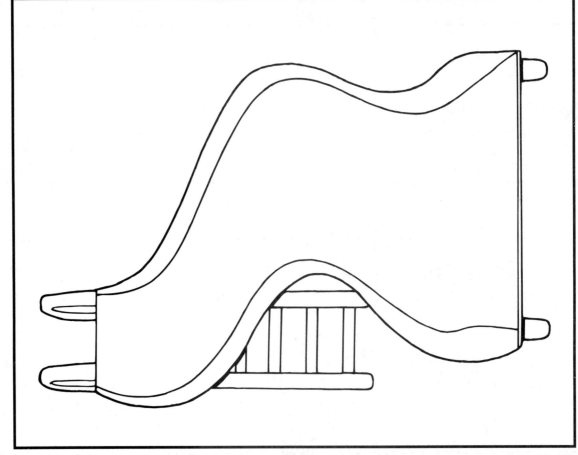

Blending Cards

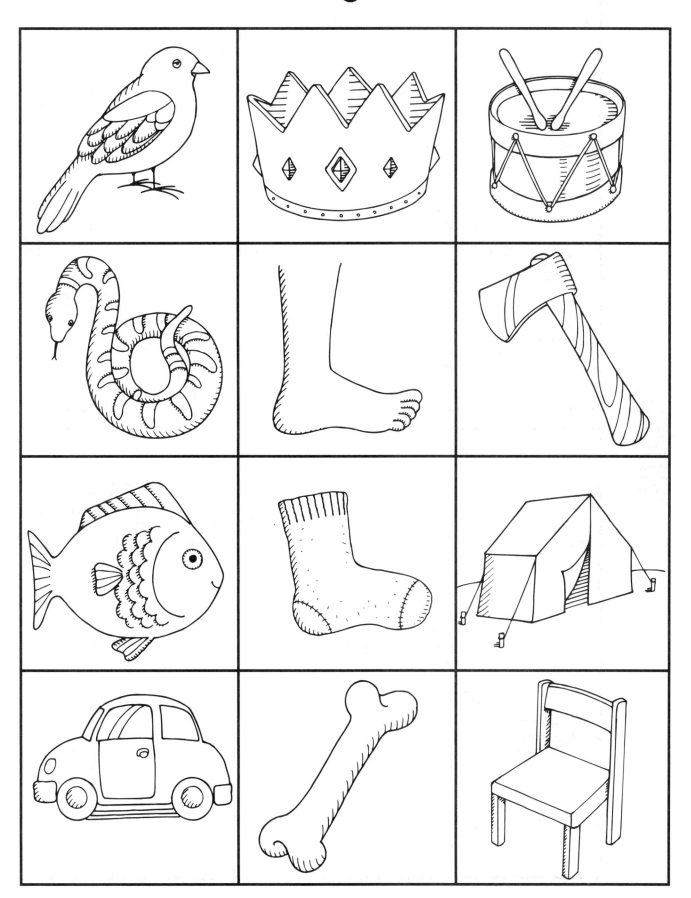

Blending Cards

Ghost Talk

Task: oral blending

Materials
☆ Ghost reproducible (page 62)
☆ Ghost Talk Strips (pages 63–64)
☆ scissors

Preparation

Copy the Ghost reproducible, cut out the ghost, laminate it, and cut a slit along the boldfaced line on the mouth. Copy and cut apart the Ghost Talk Strips, and laminate them.

- -

Ghost Talk

How to play

Place the ghost on a flat surface, and give a child a set of strips. Have the child select a strip and place it behind the ghost's head and through its mouth. Encourage the child to slowly pull the strip and name the picture, stretching out the sound until the strip is completely pulled through the ghost's mouth. Tell the child to repeat the process with the remaining strips.

❶ Self-Correcting Feature

The last sound of the word should be said as the end of the strip is pulled from the ghost's mouth.

Getting Ready to Read © 2002 Creative Teaching Press

- -

Ghost Talk

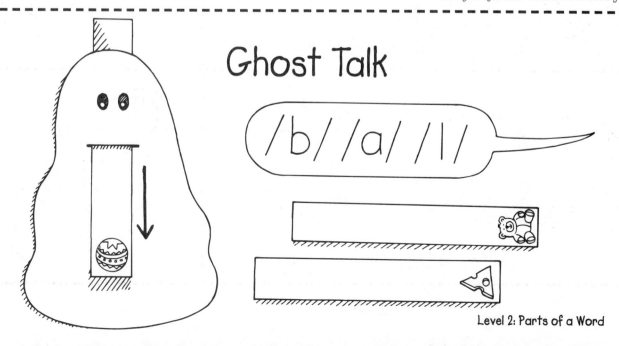

/b/ /a/ /l/

Ghost

Ghost Talk Strips

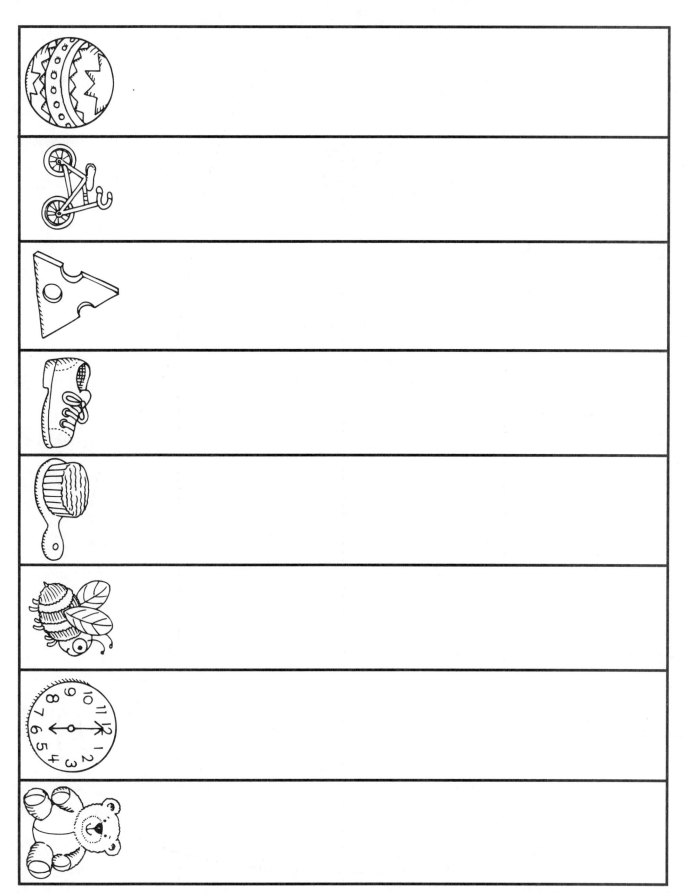

Getting Ready to Read! © 2002 Creative Teaching Press

Ghost Talk Strips

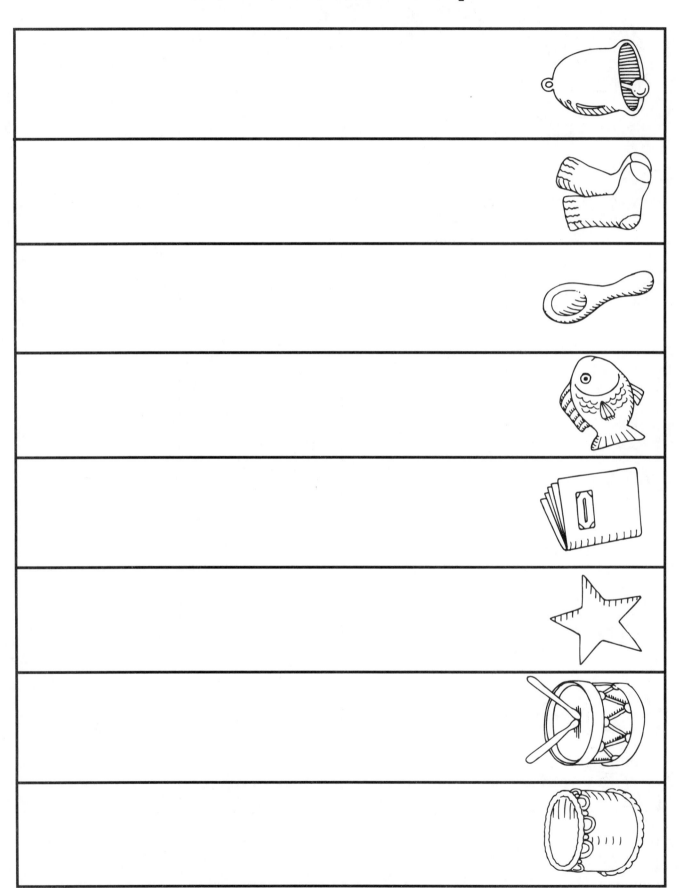

Basketball Blending

Task: oral blending

Preparation

Copy the Basketball Blending reproducible, and laminate it. Cut a slit along the boldfaced line on the basketball net. Copy and cut apart the Blending Cards, and laminate them.

Materials
☆ Basketball Blending reproducible (page 66)
☆ Blending Cards (pages 59–60)
☆ scissors

Basketball Blending

How to play

Place the Basketball Blending reproducible on a flat surface, and give a child a set of cards. Have the child select a card and place it over the basketball player. Ask the child to name the picture on the card. Tell the child to move the card along the dotted line and slowly repeat the name again until the card reaches the basket. Have the child place the card through the slot in the basket. Tell the child to repeat the process with the remaining cards.

❗ Self-Correcting Feature

The last sound of the word should be said as the card is inserted through the slot.

Getting Ready to Read © 2002 Creative Teaching Press

Basketball Blending

Basketball Blending

Elastic Words

Task: oral blending

Materials
☆ Blending Cards (pages 59–60)
☆ scissors
☆ piece of elastic

Preparation
Copy and cut apart the Blending Cards, and laminate them.

Elastic Words

How to play

Shuffle the cards, and place them facedown in a pile. Tell a child to draw a card and name the picture on it. Give the child a piece of elastic, and have him or her hold one end of the elastic in each hand. Tell the child to slowly repeat the name of the picture as he or she pulls the piece of elastic as far as it will go. Invite the child to repeat the process with the remaining cards.

❗ Self-Correcting Feature
The last sound of the word should be said as the elastic is completely stretched.

Getting Ready to Read © 2002 Creative Teaching Press

Elastic Words

All Aboard!

Task: isolating beginning sounds

Materials
☆ Train reproducible (page 69)
☆ Beginning Sound Cards (pages 70–71)
☆ scissors
☆ paper lunch sack

Preparation

Make eight copies of the Train reproducible, and cut out the trains. Write one of the following letters in each engine of a train: *b, c, d, f, g, h, j,* and *k*. Laminate the trains. Copy and cut apart the Beginning Sound Cards. Write the beginning sound of the picture on the back of each card, laminate the cards, and place them in a paper sack.

All Aboard!

Place the trains on a flat surface. Invite a child to draw a card from the paper sack and place it on a car of the train with the matching beginning sound written in the engine. For example, a child would place the duck picture card on a car of the train marked *d.* Have the child repeat the process with the remaining cards. For play with two or more children, give each player a train. Have the players sit in a semicircle and place their train beside them where everyone can see it. Invite a player to draw a card and place it on a car of the train with the matching beginning sound. Have the players repeat the process with the remaining cards. To extend the activity, copy the remaining Beginning Sound Cards (pages 72–74), and repeat the preparation process and activity with the letters *l, m, n, p, q, r, s, t, v, w, y,* and *z.*

❶ Self-Correcting Feature

The beginning sound is written on the back of each card.

Getting Ready to Read © 2002 Creative Teaching Press

All Aboard!

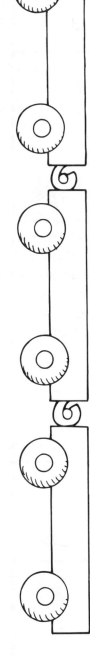

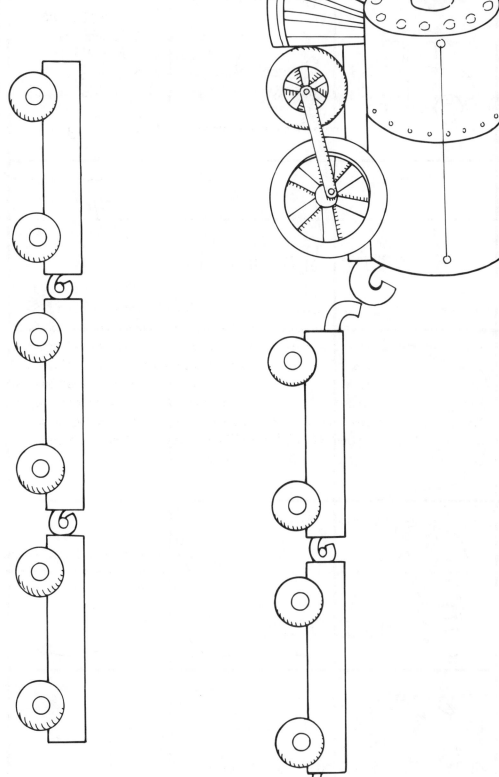

Train

Beginning Sound Cards

Beginning Sound Cards

Beginning Sound Cards

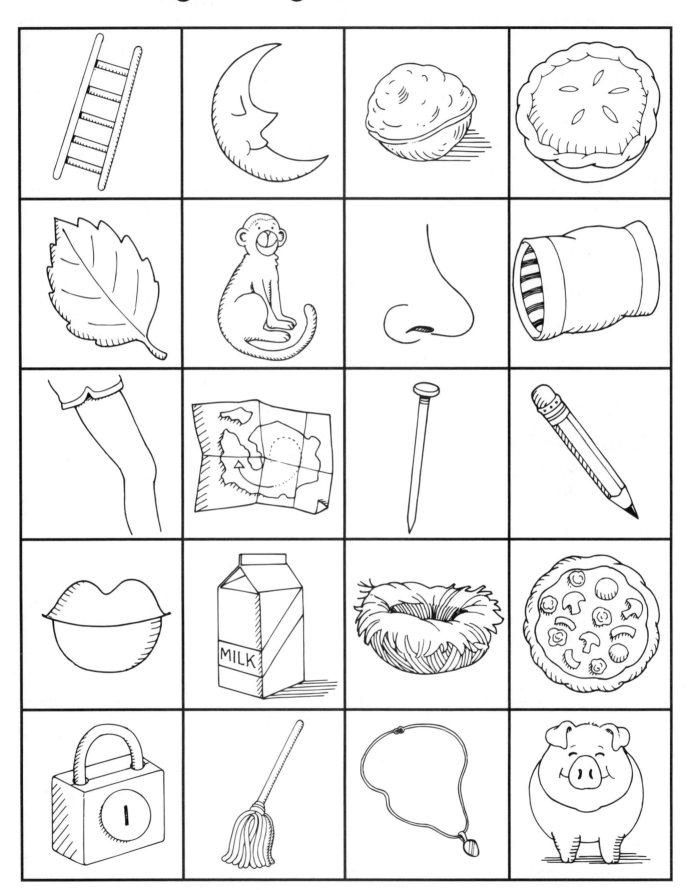

Beginning Sound Cards

Beginning Sound Cards

Picture Dominoes
Task: matching beginning sounds

Level
3

Preparation

Copy the Dominoes reproducibles, and cut apart the dominoes. Write the beginning sound for each picture on the back of each domino, and laminate the dominoes.

Picture Dominoes

How to play

Scatter the dominoes faceup on a flat surface. Ask a child to select a domino and name both pictures on it. Have the child find another domino with a picture that begins with the same sound as one of the pictures he or she just named. Tell the child to arrange the dominoes so that the matching pictures touch. Have the child select another domino with a picture that matches the beginning sound of one of the two unattached pictures. Tell the child to continue the process with the remaining dominoes. For play with two or three children, give each player six dominoes. Place the remaining dominoes in the center of the playing area, and have the players take turns placing dominoes. If a player is unable to find a match on his or her turn, he or she must pass to the next player. Have children play until they have placed all the dominoes.

❗ Self-Correcting Feature

The beginning sound of each picture is written on the back of each domino. Matching dominoes have the same letters.

Getting Ready to Read © 2002 Creative Teaching Press

Picture Dominoes

Dominoes

Dominoes

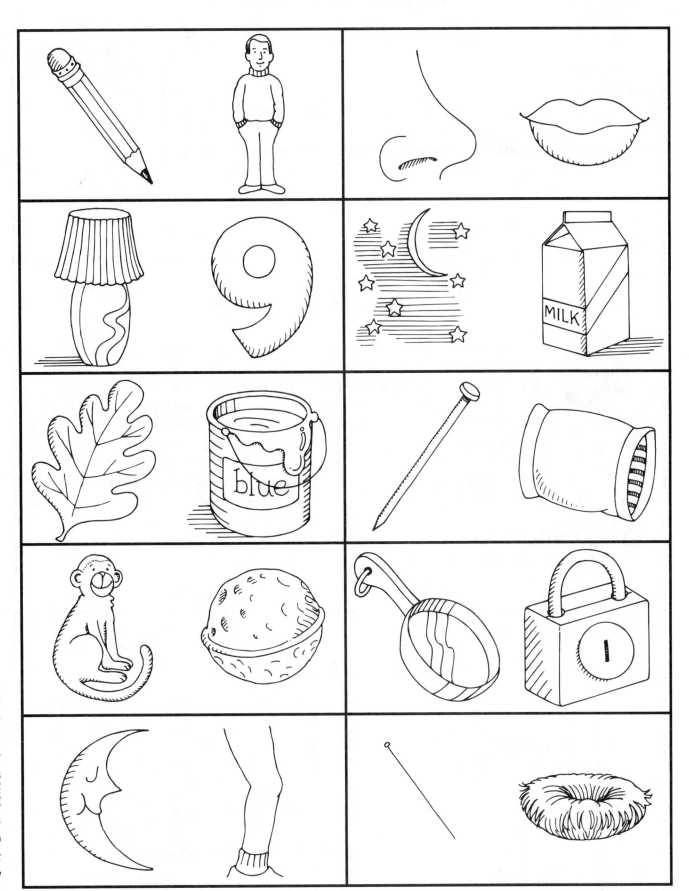

Level 3

House of Sounds
Task: isolating beginning sounds

Materials
☆ House reproducible (page 14)
☆ Beginning Sound Cards (pages 72–73)
☆ scissors
☆ paper lunch sack

Preparation
Make eight copies of the House reproducible, and cut out the houses. Write one of the following letters in each roof of a house: *l, m, n, p, q, r, s,* and *t.* Laminate the houses. Copy and cut apart the Beginning Sound Cards. Write the beginning sound of the picture on the back of each card, laminate the cards, and place them in a paper sack.

House of Sounds

How to play

Place the houses on a flat surface. Invite a child to draw a card from the paper sack and place it on the house with the matching beginning sound. For example, the picture of the leaf would be placed on the roof marked *l.* Have the child repeat the process with the remaining cards. For play with two or more children, give each player a house. Have the first player draw a card. The player may keep the card if it has the same beginning sound as the sound on the roof of his or her house and then draw again. If the sounds do not match, tell the player to place the card back in the sack and pass it to the next player. To extend the activity, copy a different set of Beginning Sound Cards (pages 70–74), and repeat the preparation process and activity with the new beginning sounds.

❗ Self-Correcting Feature
The beginning sound is written on the back of each card.

Getting Ready to Read © 2002 Creative Teaching Press

House of Sounds

Level 3

Three-in-a-Row
Task: matching beginning sounds

Materials
☆ Three-in-a-Row Cards (page 80)
☆ scissors
☆ paper lunch sack
☆ pocket chart

Preparation

Copy the Three-in-a-Row Cards, cut apart the first row of cards, and write *1* on the back of each card. Repeat this process with rows 2—4. Laminate all of the cards, and place them in a paper sack.

Three-in-a-Row

How to play

Invite a child to draw a card from the paper sack and place it in the first row of a pocket chart. Tell the child to draw another card. If the second card matches the beginning sound of the first card, have the child place it in the same row. If the beginning sounds on the two cards do not match, have the child place the card in a new row of the chart. Tell the child to repeat the process with the remaining cards. For play with two or more children, have each player draw a card until each player has a card with a different beginning sound. Tell the players to take turns drawing cards and keep only those cards that match the beginning sound on their card. Have children repeat the process with the remaining cards.

❗ Self-Correcting Feature

The three cards that have the same beginning sound have the same number on the back.

Getting Ready to Read © 2002 Creative Teaching Press

Three-in-a-Row

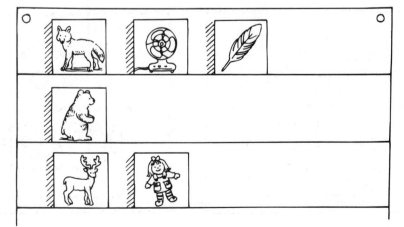

Three-in-a-Row Cards

Scavenger Hunt

Task: identifying beginning and ending sounds

Materials
- ☆ Scavenger Hunt reproducible (page 82)
- ☆ Beginning Sound Cards (pages 70–74)
- ☆ scissors
- ☆ paper lunch sack
- ☆ transparency marker

Preparation

Copy the Scavenger Hunt reproducible, and laminate it. Copy and cut apart the Beginning Sound Cards. Write on the back of each card the first letter, a blank line, and the last letter of the name of the picture. Laminate the cards, and place them in a paper sack.

Scavenger Hunt

How to play

Give a child the Scavenger Hunt reproducible. Invite the child to draw a card from the paper sack and place it over the first box on the reproducible. Tell the child to name the picture on the card and use the transparency marker to write on the reproducible the beginning and ending sounds before and after the picture. Have the child draw another card, place it on the next box, and repeat the process with the remaining cards. Ask the child to clean the reproducible.

❶ Self-Correcting Feature

The first and last letters of the word are written on the back of each card.

Getting Ready to Read © 2002 Creative Teaching Press

Scavenger Hunt

Scavenger Hunt

First or Last?

Task: matching beginning and ending sounds

Preparation

Copy the First or Last? reproducibles. Cut apart the position cards and the target letter cards, and laminate them. Cut apart each set of picture cards along the boldfaced lines. Fold each set of picture cards along the dotted line, and glue them together to create two-sided cards. Cut apart the picture cards. Write the target letter on the back of each picture card, and then laminate the cards.

Materials
☆ First or Last? reproducibles (pages 84–85)
☆ scissors
☆ glue

First or Last?

How to play

Choose a target letter. Place the matching target letter card on a flat surface, and place the two position cards below it. Give a child a set of four picture cards with the same target letter. Invite the child to look at a picture card and decide if the target letter appears at the beginning or ending of the word. Tell the child to place the picture card under the matching position card. For example, for the target letter *d*, a child would place the dog card under the beginning letter position card. Have the child repeat the process with the remaining three picture cards. For play with two children, give each player a position card. Have the players take turns choosing a picture card and placing it under the correct position card.

❗ Self-Correcting Feature

The target letter and its placement in the word are written on the back of each card.

Getting Ready to Read © 2002 Creative Teaching Press

First or Last?

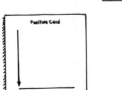

First or Last?

Position Card	Position Card

Target Letter	d	Target Letter	l

Target Letter	n	Target Letter	t

Getting Ready to Read © 2002 Creative Teaching Press

First or Last?

Mystery Picture

Task: identifying beginning and ending sounds

Materials

☆ Mystery Picture Frames reproducibles (pages 87–89)
☆ Mystery Picture Cards (page 90)
☆ scissors
☆ paper lunch sack

Preparation

Copy the Mystery Picture Frames reproducibles, cut apart the strips (rows), and laminate them. Copy and cut apart the Mystery Picture Cards. Write the first letter, a blank line, and the last letter of the name of the picture on the back of each card, and laminate the cards. Place the cards in a paper sack.

Mystery Picture

How to play

Place the strips on a flat surface. Invite a child to draw a card from the paper sack and name the picture on it. Ask the child to identify the beginning and ending sound of the word and then place the card in the center of the strip that shows those sounds. Have the child repeat the process with the remaining cards.

❶ Self-Correcting Feature

The first and last letters of the word are written on the back of each card.

Getting Ready to Read © 2002 Creative Teaching Press

Mystery Picture

Mystery Picture Frames

b		t
g		m
m		n
f		n
d		k
c		n

Getting Ready to Read© 2002 Creative Teaching Press

Mystery Picture Frames

b		g
d		s
m		t
c		n
t		k
c		t

Getting Ready to Read © 2002 Creative Teaching Press

Mystery Picture Frames

b		g
d		m
p		n
c		t
t		n
n		t

Mystery Picture Cards

Getting Ready to Read © 2002 Creative Teaching Press

Where's That Sound?

Task: approximating sounds

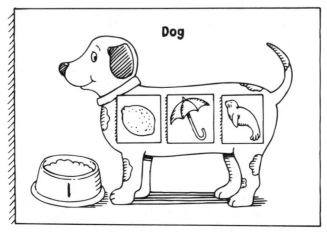

Materials
☆ Dog reproducible (page 92)
☆ Where's That Sound? Cards (page 93)
☆ scissors
☆ paper lunch sack

Preparation

Make five copies of the Dog reproducible, write *g, k, l, p* and *r* on separate dishes (one letter per dish), and laminate the papers. Copy one set of the Where's That Sound? Cards. Cut apart the first row of cards, turn over the cards, and write the target letter on the back of each one. Draw a dot below the letter to the left, middle, or right to indicate the position of the target sound, and laminate the cards. Repeat this process with the remaining rows of cards.

Where's That Sound?

How to play

Place a dog on a flat surface, and place in a paper sack all of the cards for the target letter on the dog's dish. Have a child draw a card from the sack, name the picture on it, and decide if the target letter is the beginning, middle, or ending sound of the word. Tell the child to place the card on the shoulders of the dog if it is a beginning sound, on the belly if it is a middle sound, and on the hindquarters if it is an ending sound. Invite the child to repeat this process with the three remaining cards. Repeat the activity with a new target letter and the corresponding set of cards. To extend the activity, copy the other Where's That Sound? Cards (page 94), and repeat the preparation process and activity with the letters *b, n, p, s,* and *t.*

❗ Self-Correcting Feature

The target letter and its placement in the word are written on the back of each card.

Getting Ready to Read © 2002 Creative Teaching Press

Where's That Sound?

Dog

Dog

Where's That Sound? Cards

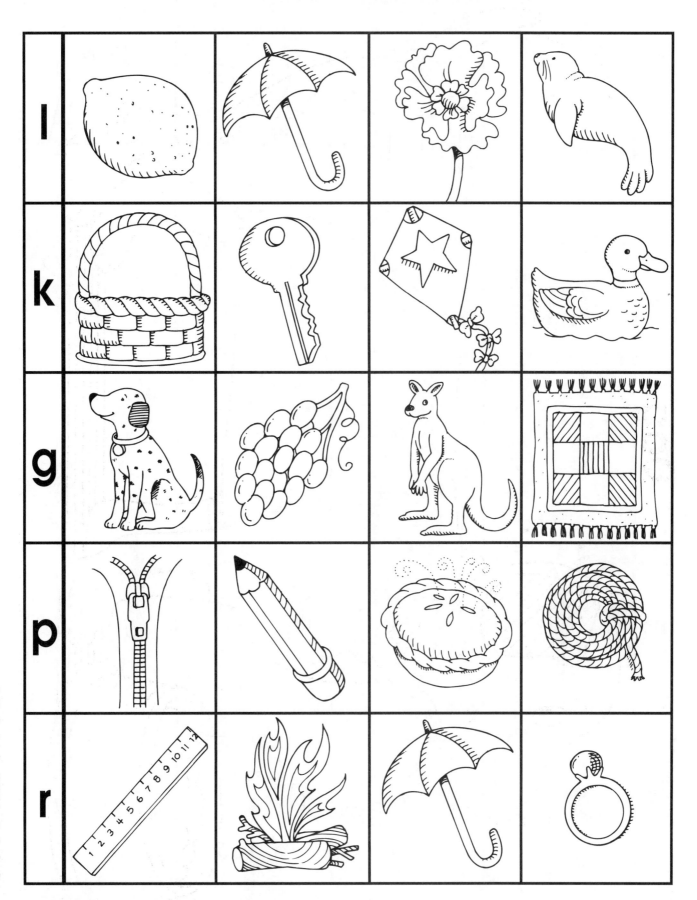

Getting Ready to Read © 2002 Creative Teaching Press

Where's That Sound? Cards

b				
s				
n				
p				
t				

Getting Ready to Read © 2002 Creative Teaching Press

Level 3

Color-Coded Sounds

Task: approximating sounds

Materials
☆ Where's That Sound? Cards (pages 93–94)
☆ scissors
☆ paper lunch sacks
☆ green, blue, and red markers
☆ index cards
☆ plastic counters

Preparation

Copy the Where's That Sound? Cards. Cut apart the cards in the first row. Turn over the cards, and write the target letter on the back of each one. Draw a dot below the letter to the left, middle, or right to indicate the position of the target sound in the word, and laminate the cards. Write the target letter on a paper sack, and place the cards in the sack. Repeat this process with the remaining sets of cards. Draw three horizontal lines—one green, one blue, and one red—along the bottom of four separate index cards. Laminate the index cards.

Color-Coded Sounds

How to play

Invite two to four children to play the game. Place a paper sack in the playing area. Give each player an index card and three counters. Have a player draw a card from the sack and name the picture on it. Ask the player to decide if the target letter (written on the sack) is the beginning, middle, or ending sound of the word. Tell the player to place the counter on the green line if it is the beginning sound, on the blue line if it is the middle sound, and on the red line if it is the ending sound. Invite the next player to draw a card and repeat the process. Tell players that if they draw a card with a sound that has already been covered on their index card, they must place the card back in the sack and pass it to the next player. Have children play until each player has covered all three lines on his or her index card. Invite children to repeat the activity with a new set of cards.

❶ Self-Correcting Feature

The target sound and its placement in the word are written on the back of each card.

Getting Ready to Read © 2002 Creative Teaching Press

Color-Coded Sounds

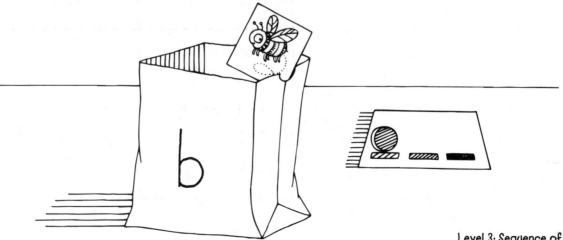

Read My Mind

Task: isolating beginning and ending sounds

Materials
☆ Read My Mind Cards (pages 97–100)
☆ scissors

Preparation
Copy the Read My Mind Cards. Make a double-sided copy of each set of cards. (Each set includes one page of picture cards and one page of sound cards.) Cut apart the cards, and laminate them.

- -

Read My Mind

How to play

Invite two or more children to play this game. Shuffle the cards (with the pictures faceup), and place them in a pile. Ask a player to draw the top three cards and place them faceup on a flat surface. Tell the player to silently choose one of the cards and give the other players clues about the beginning and ending sounds in the picture's name. For example, for the bat picture card, a player could say *I'm thinking of a word that begins with /b/ and ends with /t/.* Invite the other players to guess the word. The player who guesses the word takes the card, draws a new one from the pile, and places it faceup beside the other two cards. Ask this player to select the new secret word and give clues about it. Have the children repeat the process with the remaining cards.

❗ Self-Correcting Feature
The beginning and ending sounds for the name of the picture are written on the back of each card.

Getting Ready to Read © 2002 Creative Teaching Press

- -

Read My Mind

I'm thinking of a word that begins with /t/ and ends with /n/.

Read My Mind Cards—Set 1

Read My Mind Cards—Set I

r_n	b_t	p_n
p_g	t_n	s_n
n_t	b_k	c_k
cl_k	p_t	c_t

Getting Ready to Read © 2002 Creative Teaching Press

Read My Mind Cards—Set II

Read My Mind Cards—Set II

f_r	f_t	l_t
t_p	m_k	l_n
k_n	n_t	m_n
b_l	h_s	l_k

Penny Push
Task: matching sounds

Materials
☆ Penny Push repro-
   ducible (page 102)
☆ Penny Push Word
   Cards (page 103)
☆ scissors
☆ paper lunch sack
☆ pennies

Preparation

Copy the Penny Push reproducible, cut apart the strips, and laminate them.
Copy and cut apart the Penny Push Word Cards. Write the number of sounds
(not letters) in the word (e.g., *ladder* has four sounds, /l/ /a/ /d/ /r/) on the
back of each card. Laminate the cards, and place them in a paper sack.

- -

Penny Push

How to play

Give a child a strip and four pennies. Invite the child to draw a card from the paper sack and
place it above his or her strip. Ask the child to slowly name the picture on the card and place a
penny in a separate box for each sound he or she says. For example, a child would place four
pennies as he or she says /h/ /a/ /n/ /d/ for *hand*. Invite the child to repeat the process
with the remaining cards.

❗ Self-Correcting Feature

The number of sounds in the name of the picture is written on the back of each card.

Getting Ready to Read © 2002 Creative Teaching Press

- -

Penny Push

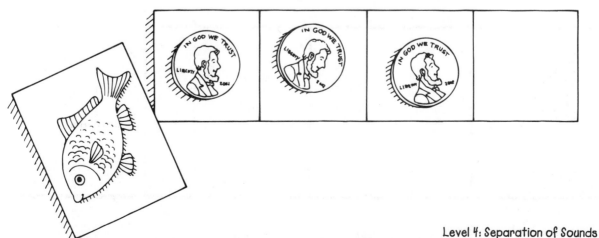

Penny Push

Getting Ready to Read © 2002 Creative Teaching Press

Penny Push Word Cards

Count the Sounds
Task: counting sounds

Materials
- ☆ Graph reproducible (page 40)
- ☆ Counting Sounds Cards (pages 105–106)
- ☆ tape
- ☆ scissors
- ☆ paper lunch sack

Preparation

Make two copies of the Graph reproducible, and tape them together to make four columns of eight. Label below the bottom rows from 1 to 4, and laminate the graph. Copy and cut apart the Counting Sounds Cards. Write the number of sounds (not letters) in the word (e.g., *knee* has two sounds, /n/ /ē/) on the back of each card. Laminate the cards, and place them in a paper sack.

Count the Sounds

How to play

Place the graph on a flat surface. Invite a child to draw a card from the paper sack, name the picture, and decide how many individual sounds are in the word. For example, a child selects the card with the baby picture, says /b/ /a/ /b/ /y/, and identifies that there are four sounds in the word. Tell the child to place the card in the column on the graph with the matching number. Have the child repeat the process with the remaining cards. For play with two or more children, give each player a graph. Invite the players to take turns drawing cards and placing them on their graph according to the number of sounds in the words. Tell players that if they select a card with a number of sounds they have already covered on their graph, they must place the card back in the sack and pass it to the next player. Have the children play until each child has placed a card above all four numbers on his or her graph.

❗ Self-Correcting Feature

The number of sounds in the name of the picture is written on the back of each card.

Getting Ready to Read © 2002 Creative Teaching Press

Count the Sounds

Counting Sounds Cards

Counting Sounds Cards

Towers of Sounds
Task: segmenting sounds

Materials
☆ Counting Sounds Cards (pages 105–106)
☆ scissors
☆ paper lunch sack
☆ linking cubes

Preparation

Copy and cut apart the Counting Sounds Cards. Write the number of sounds (not letters) in the word (e.g., *knee* has two sounds, /n/ /ē/) on the back of each card. Laminate the cards, and place them in a paper sack.

Towers of Sounds

How to play

Invite a child to draw a card from the paper sack. Tell the child to draw cards and place them back in the sack until he or she draws a card with a picture that has two sounds in the name. Have the child connect two linking cubes, and place the two-cube "tower" beside the card. Tell the child to draw another card and place it back in the sack until he or she draws a card with a picture that has three sounds in the name. Have him or her build a three-cube tower. Invite the child to repeat the process with four- and five-sound words. For play with two or more children, have the players take turns drawing a card and building individual towers in sequence.

❗ Self-Correcting Feature

The number of sounds in the name of the picture is written on the back of each card.

Getting Ready to Read © 2002 Creative Teaching Press

Towers of Sounds

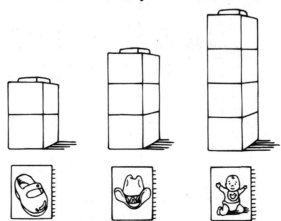

Level 4

Sound Sorting Houses

Task: counting sounds

Materials
☆ More Counting Sounds Cards (pages 109–110)
☆ House reproducible (page 14)
☆ scissors
☆ paper lunch sack

Preparation

Copy and cut apart the More Counting Sounds Cards. Write the number of sounds (not letters) in the word (e.g., *tie* has two sounds, /t/ /ī/) on the back of each card. Laminate the cards, and place them in a paper sack. Make four copies of the House reproducible. Write numbers from 2–5 on the roof of each house, and laminate the houses.

Sound Sorting Houses

Place the houses on a flat surface. Invite a child to draw a card from the paper sack, identify the number of sounds in the word, and place it in the house with the matching number. For example, if a child picks the pin picture card, he or she would place it on the house marked *3*. Have the child repeat the process with the remaining cards. For play with two or more children, give each player a house. Have the first player draw a card. If the picture on the card has the same number of sounds as the number on his or her house, he or she may keep the card and draw another card. If the card does not have the same number of sounds, the player places the card back in the sack, and the next player takes a turn. Have children repeat the process with the remaining cards.

❗ Self-Correcting Feature

The number of sounds in the name of the picture is written on the back of each card.

Getting Ready to Read © 2002 Creative Teaching Press

Sound Sorting Houses

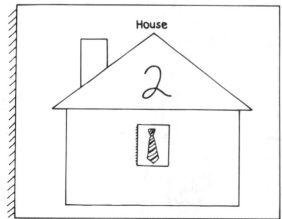

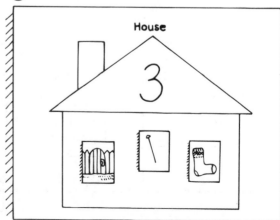

More Counting Sounds Cards

More Counting Sounds Cards

Spin and Take
Task: counting sounds

Materials
☆ More Counting Sounds Cards (pages 109–110)
☆ number spinner (page 112)
☆ scissors
☆ brass fastener

Preparation

Copy and cut apart the More Counting Sounds Cards. Write the number of sounds (not letters) in the word (e.g., *tie* has two sounds, /t/ /ī/) on the back of each card, and laminate the cards. Copy and cut out the number spinner and arrow, and laminate them. (Use the letter spinner for the activity on page 131.) Use a brass fastener to attach the arrow to the center of the spinner.

Spin and Take

Scatter the cards faceup on a flat surface. Invite a child to spin the spinner and find a card with a matching number of sounds. Have the child repeat the process with the remaining cards. For play with two or more children, have each player take turns spinning the spinner and taking a card with a matching number of sounds. When a player spins a number and a card with that number of sounds is no longer available, the player passes to the next player. Have children repeat the process with the remaining cards.

❗ Self-Correcting Feature

The number of sounds in the name of the picture is written on the back of each card.

Getting Ready to Read © 2002 Creative Teaching Press

Spin and Take

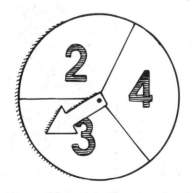

Spinners

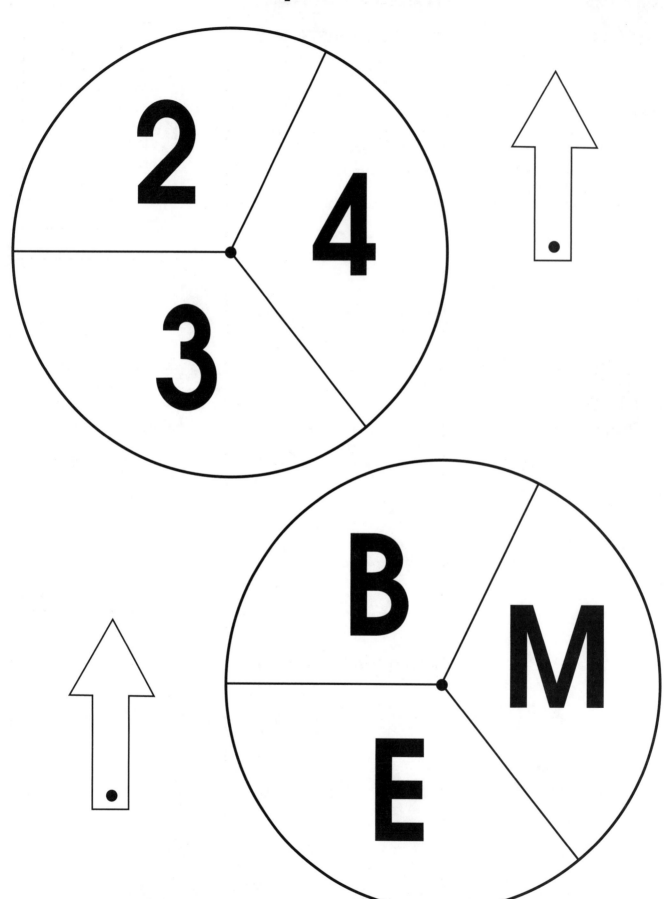

Level 4

Number Race
Task: counting sounds

Materials
☆ Number Race repro-
  ducible (page 114)
☆ More Counting
  Sounds Cards
  (pages 109–110)
☆ scissors
☆ paper lunch sack
☆ game markers

Preparation

Make four copies of the the Number Race reproducible, and laminate them. Copy and cut apart the More Counting Sounds Cards. Write the number of sounds (not letters) in the word (e.g., *tie* has two sounds, /t/ /ī/) on the back of each card. Laminate the cards, and place them in a paper sack.

Number Race

How to play

Invite two to four children to play this game. Give each player a Number Race reproducible and a game marker. Tell the children to place their game marker on "Start." Invite a player to draw a card, name the picture, and decide how many sounds are in the word. Tell the player to place his or her marker on the first number after "Start" that matches the number of sounds in his or her word. Ask the next player to draw a card and repeat the process. Tell the players that if the number they are looking for is not available in front of their marker, they must move back-wards to the number. Have children continue the activity until each player reaches "Stop."

❶ Self-Correcting Feature

The number of sounds in the name of the picture is written on the back of each card.

Getting Ready to Read © 2002 Creative Teaching Press

Number Race

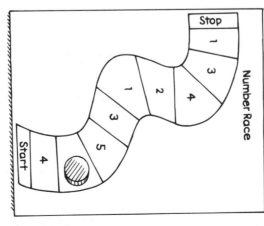

Number Race

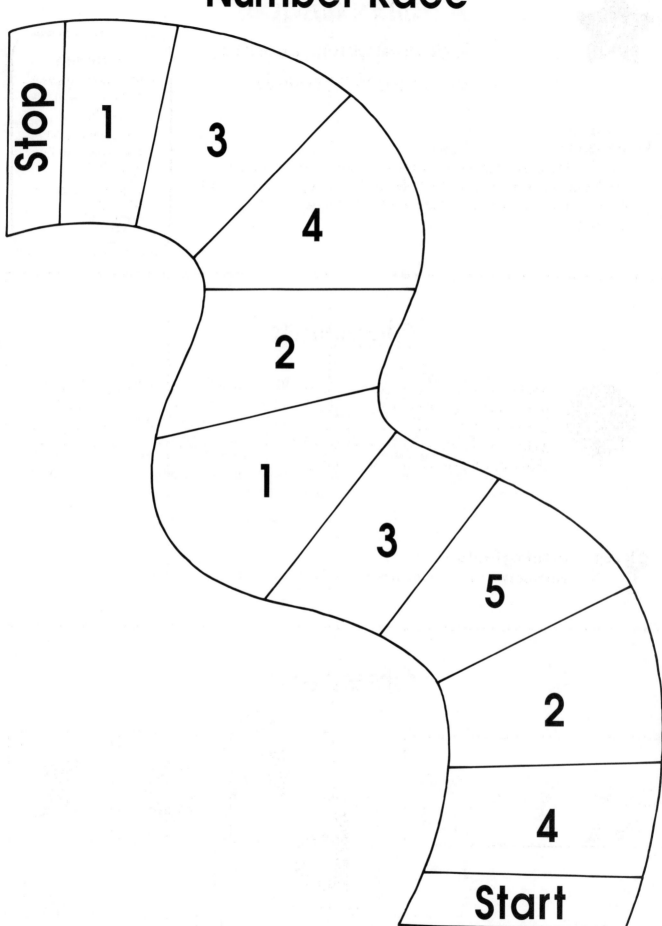

Change It

Task: manipulating beginning and ending sounds

Materials
☆ Change the Beginning Sound reproducible (page 116)
☆ Change the Ending Sound reproducible (page 117)
☆ Letter Cards (pages 53–54)
☆ scissors

Preparation
Copy the Change the Beginning Sound and Change the Ending Sound reproducibles, and cut apart the strips. Write the word for both pictures on the back of the strips, and laminate them. Copy and cut apart the Letter Cards, and laminate them.

Change It

How to play

Shuffle the strips, and place them faceup in a pile. Scatter the letter cards faceup around the pile. Invite a child to draw a strip and place it on a flat surface. Have the child name the first picture on the strip, and use the letter cards to spell the word. Ask the child to name the second picture, decide which sound is different, and change a letter to make the new word. Have the child repeat the process with the remaining strips.

❶ **Self-Correcting Feature**
The cards have both picture words written on the back.

Getting Ready to Read © 2002 Creative Teaching Press

Change It

Change the Beginning Sound

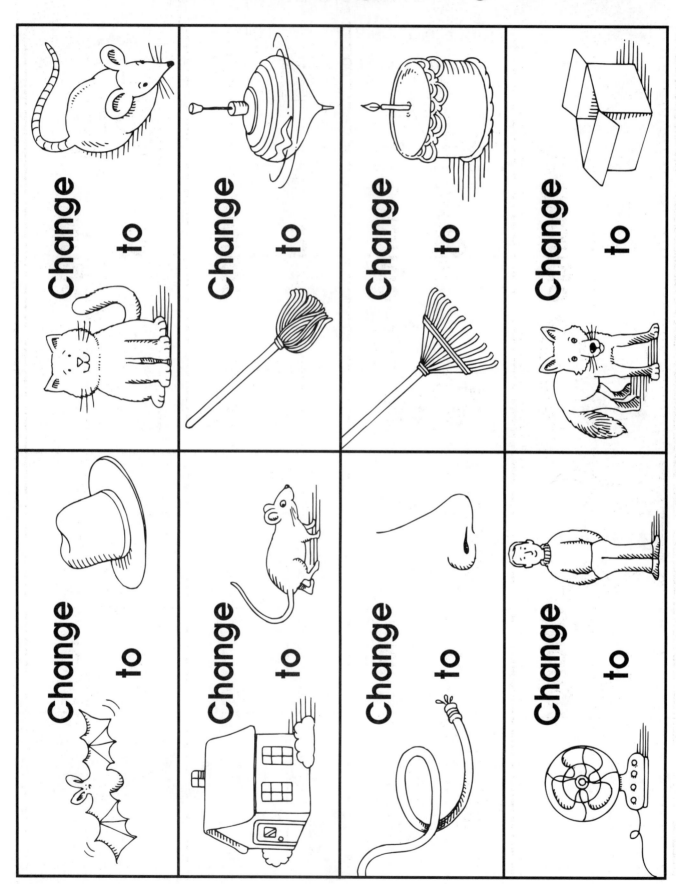

Change the Ending Sound

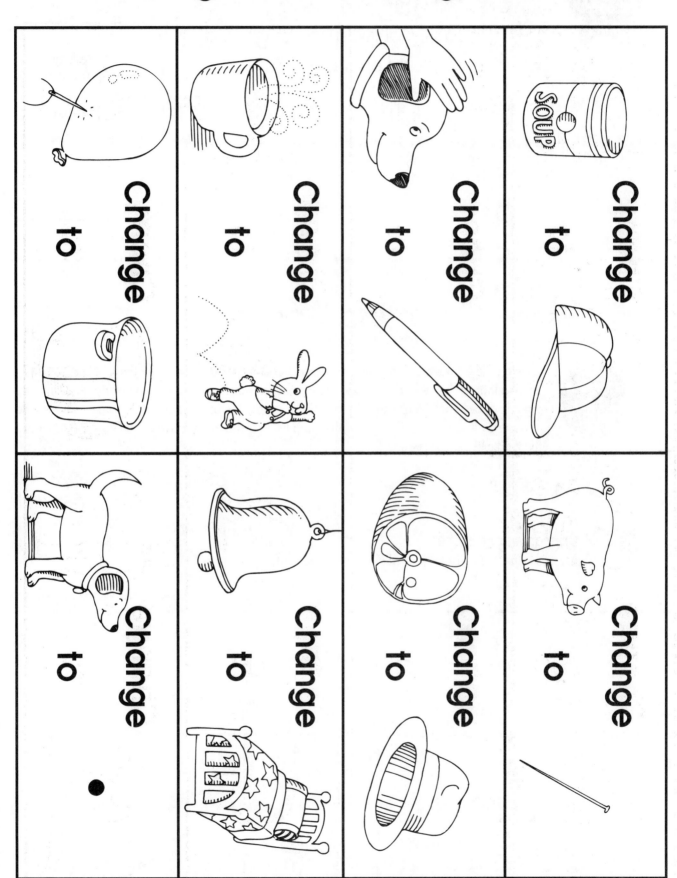

Zigzag Words
Task: manipulating beginning and ending sounds

Materials
☆ Zigzag Words reproducibles (pages 119–120)
☆ scissors
☆ paper clips
☆ transparency marker

Preparation
Copy the Zigzag Words reproducibles, cut them apart along the thick lines, and laminate them. Fold back the word lists, and clip them together.

Zigzag Words

How to play

Give a child a folded zigzag card, and have him or her read the word on the first line. Tell the child to look at the second word and use a transparency marker to write the letter that appears directly above each blank line. Ask the child to repeat the process until he or she has made nine new words. Invite the child to unfold the word list and check the answers. Tell the child to clean the card and pick a new one.

❗ **Self-Correcting Feature**
The words in the lists on both sides of the card should match.

Getting Ready to Read © 2002 Creative Teaching Press

Zigzag Words

s	i	t
b	i̱	ṯ
ḇ	i̱	g
p	i̱	g
p̱	i̱	n

Zigzag Words

Zigzag Words

fun sun sum gum gut but bud mud mum hum

f u n | s _ | m _ | g _ | t _ | b _ | d _ | m _ | m _ | h _

cap map man pan pad sad sap nap nab cab

c a p | m _ | n _ | _ | p _ | d _ | s _ | p _ | n _ | b _ | c _

Criss-Cross Words

Task: manipulating beginning and ending sounds

Materials
☆ Criss-Cross Word Cards (pages 122–123)
☆ scissors
☆ glue
☆ transparency marker

Preparation
Copy the Criss-Cross Word Cards, and cut apart the cards along the thick lines. Cut apart the strip of words above each card, glue it to the back of the card, and laminate the cards.

- -

Criss-Cross Words

How to play

Give a child a Criss-Cross Word Card, and tell him or her to read the sounds and words along both sides. Invite the child to look at the first word on the card and use a transparency marker to draw a line to connect the word to a sound that would change the beginning of the word to make a new word. For example, a child could connect the *w* to *tag* to make *wag*. Tell the child to connect the other two sounds to make two additional words. Ask the child to clean the card, pick a new one, and repeat the activity.

❗ Self-Correcting Feature
A list of the new words is on the back of each card.

Getting Ready to Read © 2002 Creative Teaching Press

- -

Criss-Cross Words

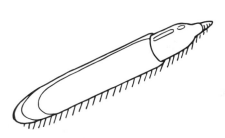

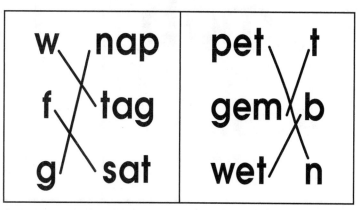

Criss-Cross Word Cards

wag, fat, gap	pen, get, web
w nap	pet t
f tag	gem b
g sat	wet n

job, top, not	cup, bug, bun
j mop	cut n
t mob	but p
n lot	bus g

Criss-Cross Word Cards

den, get, red	dot, rod, pop
d men	dog p
g fed	rob t
r pet	pot d

fun, jug, cub	dig, wit, skim
f dug	did t
j bun	wig m
c tub	skin g

Word Puzzles

Task: manipulating beginning and ending sounds

Materials
☆ Word Puzzles (pages 125–126)
☆ Word Puzzles Lists (page 127)
☆ scissors
☆ envelopes
☆ tape

Preparation

Copy the Word Puzzles and Word Puzzles Lists. Cut apart the pieces in column 1 on the Word Puzzles, write *1* on the back of each piece, and laminate the pieces. Write the word *bad* and the number *1* on an envelope, and place the pieces inside the envelope. Cut out the corresponding list, and tape it to the back of the envelope. Repeat this process with the remaining seven sets of pieces and their corresponding word list using 2–8.

- -

Word Puzzles

How to play

Give a child an envelope, and ask him or her to remove the pieces. Ask the child to read the word on the envelope and connect the pieces to make that word. Tell the child to change one of the pieces to make a new word and write the new word on a piece of paper. Have the child continue changing letters and writing as many new words as he or she can. Tell the child to compare his or her list with the list on the envelope. Have the child return the pieces to the envelope, pick a new one, and repeat the activity.

❗ Self-Correcting Feature

A list of words appears on the back of each envelope.

Getting Ready to Read © 2002 Creative Teaching Press

- -

Word Puzzles

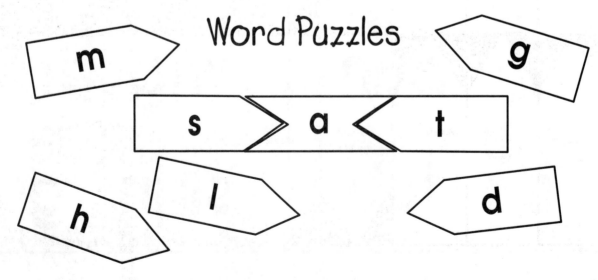

Word Puzzles

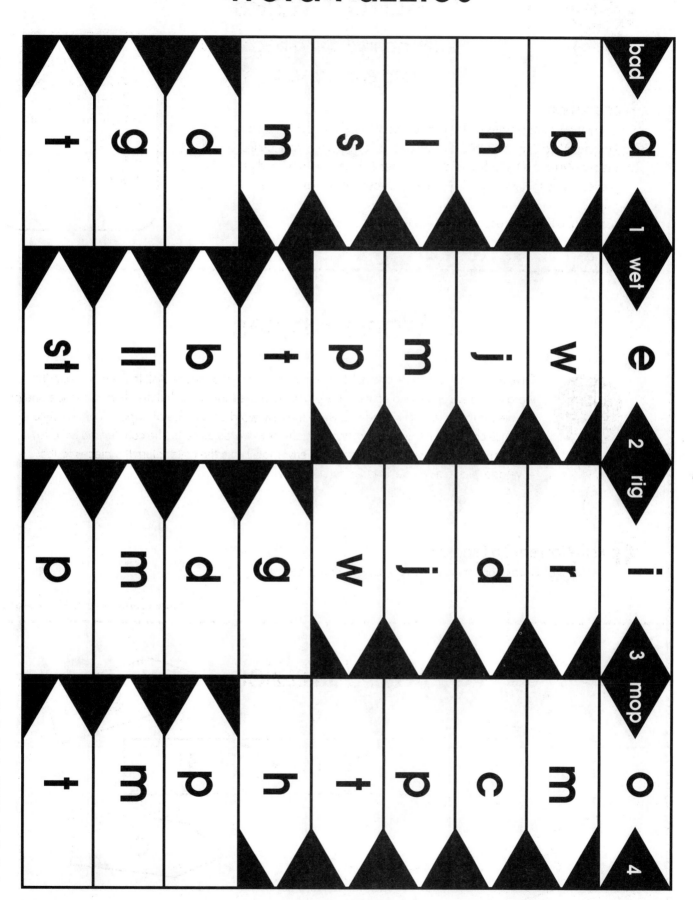

Word Puzzles

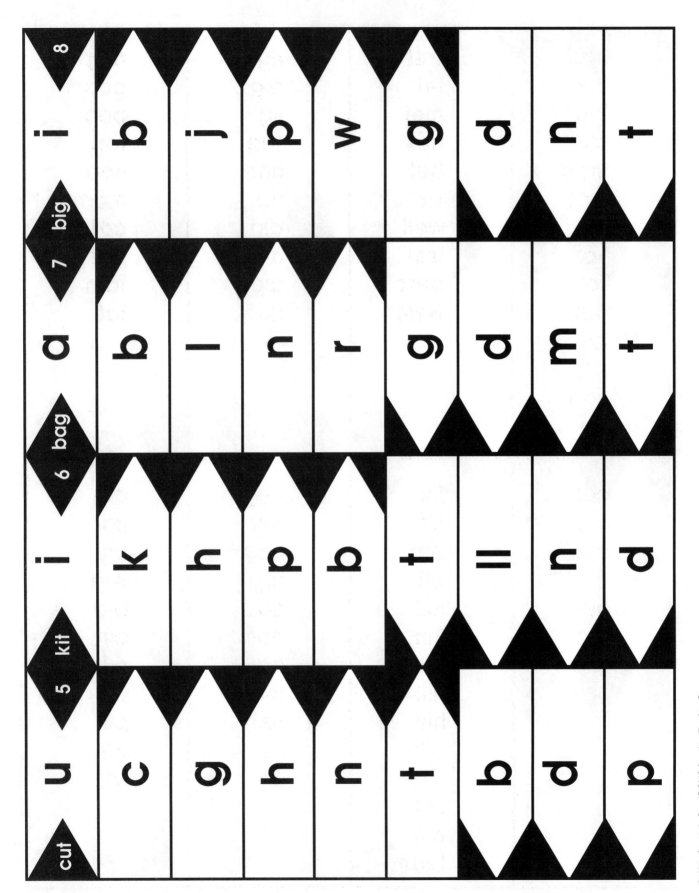

Word Puzzles Lists

bad	**wet**	**rig**	**mop**
had	jet	dig	cop
lad	met	jig	pop
sad	pet	wig	top
mad	bet	rim	hop
mat	web	rid	mom
bag	well	did	cot
hat	jest	dim	pot
sat	pest	dip	tom
bat	west	rip	tot
lag			
sag			
hag			

cut	**kit**	**bag**	**big**
cub	hit	lag	jig
cud	pit	nag	pig
cup	bit	rag	wig
gut	kill	bad	bid
hut	kin	bam	bin
hub	kid	bat	bit
	hill	lad	pin
	hid	ram	pit
	pill	rat	win
	pin		wit
	bill		
	bin		
	bid		

Now It Says

Task: manipulating beginning and ending sounds

Materials
☆ Now It Says reproducibles (pages 129–130)
☆ green and red crayons or markers
☆ scissors
☆ envelopes

Preparation

Copy the Now It Says reproducibles. Look at the first word. Color the letter cards to the left of the word green, and color the letter cards to the right of the word red. Cut apart the word card and the corresponding letter cards, and write *1* on the back of each card. Laminate all the cards. Write the word and *1* on an envelope, and place the pieces inside the envelope. Repeat this process with the remaining seven sets of words and their letter cards using numbers 2–8.

Now It Says

Give a child an envelope, and ask him or her to remove the cards. Tell the child that the green letters are beginning letters and the red letters are ending letters. Invite the child to read the word on the card. Then, have the child change one beginning or ending letter, say *Now it says*, and read aloud the new word. Invite the child to use different beginning and ending letters to make as many words as he or she can. Invite the child to return the word and letter cards to the envelope, pick a new one, and repeat the activity.

❶ Self-Correcting Feature

Any combination of first or last letters makes a real word.

Getting Ready to Read © 2002 Creative Teaching Press

Now It Says

Now It Says

b	f	h	cat	b	n	p
f	t	w	pin	g	ll	t
f	l	w	bed	g	ll	t
h	m	s	bad	ck	g	t

Now It Says

b	h	r	did	g	m	p
h	p	st	mop	b	d	m
m	s	t	cap	n	st	t
d	p	r	big	d	n	t

Getting Ready to Read © 2002 Creative Teaching Press

Spin a New Word
Task: manipulating sounds

Materials
☆ Spin a New Word Cards (page 132)
☆ letter spinner (page 112)
☆ scissors
☆ brass fastener

Preparation
Copy and cut apart the Spin a New Word Cards, and laminate them. Copy and cut out the letter spinner and arrow, and laminate them. (Use the number spinner for the activity on page 111.) Use a brass fastener to attach the arrow to the center of the spinner.

Spin a New Word

Invite a small group of children to play this game. Shuffle the cards, and place them facedown in a pile. Invite a player to draw a card and read it aloud. Ask the player to spin the spinner to learn whether he or she should change the beginning (B), middle (M), or ending (E) of the word. Tell the player to change the sound indicated by the arrow and say the new word. For example, a player could change the word *cat* to *bat, cut,* or *cap* depending upon the direction on the arrow. Invite a different player to draw a new card and spin the spinner. Have children repeat the process with the remaining cards.

❶ Self-Correcting Feature
The children in the group will recognize when a real word is made.

Getting Ready to Read © 2002 Creative Teaching Press

Spin a New Word

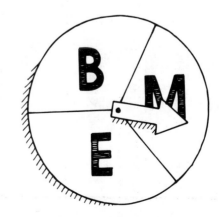

Spin a New Word Cards

cat	map	sat
bed	pen	big
win	bit	dug
cub	hum	run

Getting Ready to Read © 2002 Creative Teaching Press

Start and Stop
Task: manipulating beginning and ending sounds

Materials
☆ Start and Stop reproducibles (pages 134–135)
☆ scissors
☆ envelopes

Preparation
Copy the Start and Stop reproducibles, and cut each paper in half along the thick line. Cut apart the first set of cards, and write *1* on the back of each card. Laminate the cards, and place them in an envelope labeled *1*. Repeat this process with the remaining three sets of cards using numbers 2–4.

- -

Start and Stop

How to play

Give a child an envelope, and ask him or her to remove the cards and place them faceup on a flat surface. Ask the child to find the word card and read it aloud. Tell the child to find a card that he or she can connect to the last letter of the word to make a new word. Have the child continue attaching cards to the last letter of the new word until no cards remain. Invite the child to place all the cards back in the envelope, pick a new one, and repeat the activity.

❗ Self-Correcting Feature
The last word should match the first word.

Getting Ready to Read © 2002 Creative Teaching Press

- -

Start and Stop

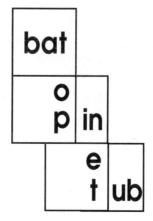

Start and Stop

bat	o p	mop	i g
in	e t	um	a n
ub	a d	ot	e n
im	a n	ab	u m
ab	a t	om	o p

Getting Ready to Read © 2002 Creative Teaching Press

Start and Stop

nut	e n	map	i n
ap	i n	ut	a g
ot	u b	et	e n
at	o p	ip	e g
an	u t	um	a p

Star Power

Task: manipulating vowels

Materials
☆ Star Power reproducible (page 137)
☆ scissors
☆ colored marker

Preparation

Make four copies of the Star Power reproducible, cut apart the cards, and use a colored marker to write one of the following words in the center of each star: *bad, clock, bag, pan, pat, tan, jag, pack, sack, tack, ham, bat, rad, hat, ball,* and *lack*. On the back of each star, write a list of three real words a child could create by changing the vowel in the center word. For example, the list on the back of the star labeled *bad* would read *bed, bid, bud*. Laminate the stars.

- - - - - - - - - - - - - - - - - - - -

Star Power

How to play

Shuffle the cards, and place them faceup in a pile. Invite a child to draw a card and read the word in the center of the star. Tell the child to write the word on a piece of paper and underline it. Have the child use three of the vowels in the points of the star to make three different real words. Ask the child to read the new words aloud and then write them on the paper. Invite the child to repeat the process with the remaining cards. For play with four children, have the first player draw a card, read the word in the center of the star, and pass the card to the next player. Ask the next player to change the middle sound of the word to make a new word and then pass it to the next player. Have players repeat the process until each player has handled the card and named a real word. Invite the last player to draw a new card and repeat the activity.

🛈 Self-Correcting Feature

A sample list of the new words is printed on the back of each card.

Getting Ready to Read © 2002 Creative Teaching Press

- - - - - - - - - - - - - - - - - - - -

Star Power

Star Power

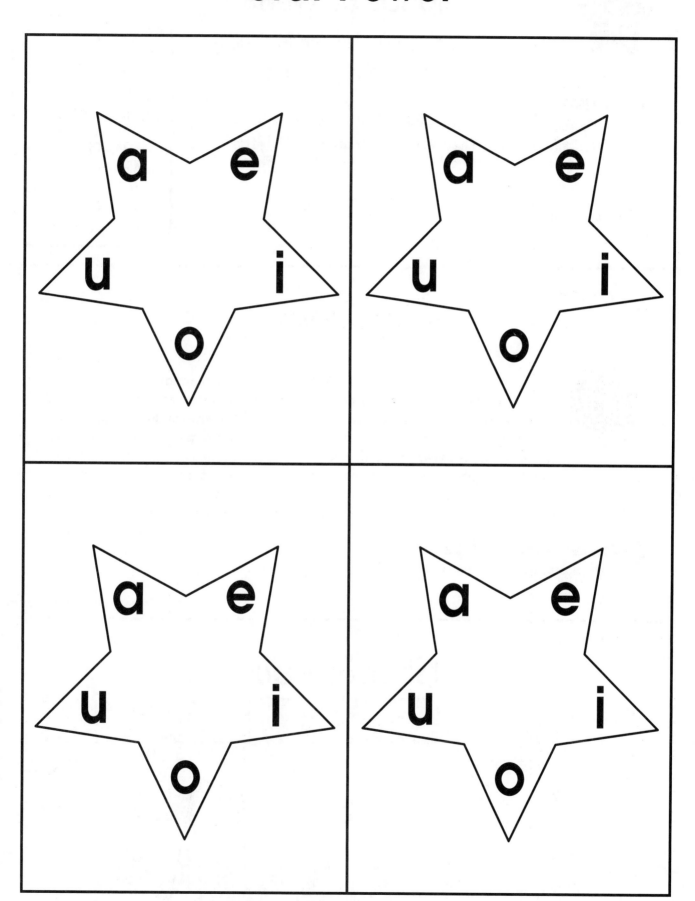

Alphabet House

Task: manipulating beginning and ending sounds

Materials
☆ House reproducible (page 14)
☆ Letter Cards (pages 53–54)
☆ Alphabet House Word Cards (pages 139–140)
☆ Alphabet House Word Lists (page 141)
☆ scissors
☆ envelopes

Preparation
Copy the House reproducible, and laminate it. Copy and cut apart several sets of Letter Cards, and laminate them. Copy and cut apart the Alphabet House Word Cards and Alphabet House Word Lists, and laminate them. Place each word card, corresponding letter cards (as indicated in the Use These Letters column next to each word card), and the corresponding word list in an envelope. Repeat this process with the remaining word cards.

- -

Alphabet House

How to play

Give a child a house and an envelope. Tell the child to place the word card above the roof of the house and the letter cards in the house. Ask the child to read the word card and use the letters cards to spell the word in the roof of the house. Then, have the child change the first, middle, and last letters to create new words, write the new words on a piece of paper, and compare the words on his or her list with the list in the envelope. Have the child place the cards back in the envelope, pick a new one, and repeat the activity.

❗ Self-Correcting Feature
All possible words appear on the word list.

Getting Ready to Read © 2002 Creative Teaching Press

- -

Alphabet House

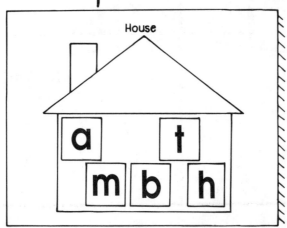

Alphabet House Word Cards

rug	**Use These Letters:** r u g m a b h t
bag	**Use These Letters:** b a g w r i d f p
nut	**Use These Letters:** n u t r h b c e g
hot	**Use These Letters:** h o t p n a c d g
bit	**Use These Letters:** b i t s p a f h l

Alphabet House Word Cards

dog	**Use These Letters:** d o g r b i j
bed	**Use These Letters:** b e d t r a f g l
cub	**Use These Letters:** c u b t a g r s
can	**Use These Letters:** c a n t r f i m p
bid	**Use These Letters:** b i d s a h l r

Alphabet House Word Lists

<u>rug</u>

rag	bag	tag	bug
hug	tug	mug	rub
rut	bat	hat	rat
mat	tab	ham	ram

<u>dog</u>

bog	jog	dig	big
jig	rig	job	rob
rib			

<u>bag</u>

big	dig	fig	pig
rig	wig	bad	bar
rag	wag	dip	rip
rid			

<u>bed</u>

bad	fad	lad	tad
fed	led	red	beg
leg	bet	let	bag
rag	tag	bar	far
tar	bat	rat	

<u>nut</u>

but	cut	hut	rut
gut	net	bet	get
hug	rug	rub	

<u>cub</u>

cab	rub	sub	tub
car	cat	rat	sat
rug	tug	gut	rut

<u>hot</u>

hat	cat	pat	cot
dot	not	pot	hog
had	got	can	pan
nag			

<u>can</u>

fan	man	pan	ran
tan	cap	cat	mat
pat	rat	fat	fin
pin	tin	rip	tip
rim	fit	pit	

<u>bit</u>

bat	fat	hat	pat
sat	fit	hit	lit
pit	sit	sip	sap
lap	has		

<u>bid</u>

bad	had	lad	sad
hid	lid	rid	bar

Flip-Flop Books

Task: matching rhyming words

Materials
☆ Flip-Flop Books
   reproducibles
   (pages 143–144)
☆ plastic binding
   machine/binding

Preparation

Copy the Flip-Flop Books reproducibles. Cut apart the first strip (with the word *cat* and the letters *m, r, p,* and *n*), and laminate the strip. Cut out the *m* and *r* letter cards, and place them over the *c* in *cat*. Cut out the *p* and *n* cards, place them over the *t* in *cat*. Bind the strips together. Repeat this process with the remaining seven strips of word and letter cards to create eight separate flip-flop books.

Flip-Flop Books

How to play

Give a child a flip-flop book, and tell him or her to flip to the word on the last page. Invite the child to flip the flaps in the last column to change the ending sound of the word. Tell the child to read aloud each new word he or she makes. Have the child flip back to the word again and then flip the flaps in the first column to change the beginning sound of the word. Invite the child to pick a new book and repeat the activity.

❗ **Self-Correcting Feature**

Any combination of letters makes a real word.

Getting Ready to Read © 2002 Creative Teaching Press

Flip-Flop Books

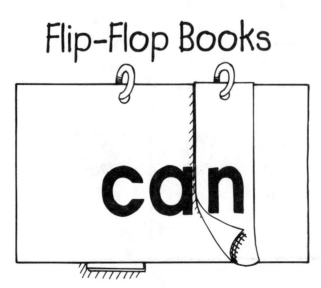

Flip-Flop Books

m	**r**	**cat**	**p**	**n**
c	**b**	**mop**	**b**	**d**
r	**h**	**bug**	**t**	**m**
m	**f**	**bad**	**t**	**n**

Flip-Flop Books

l n	cap	t b
b w	fit	n g
r b	hum	t g
f w	pin	g t